The Piccolo Coo[k]

The new Piccolo Cookbo[ok] recipes

Toad-in-the-hole
Hamburgers
Egg Salad

Poached haddock
Iced lollies
Cheese dreams
Cauliflower cheese
Orange baked bananas
Laying the table for tea
Oatmeal scones

Chocolate walnut sundae
Orange and cottage cheese salad
Omelettes
Kneading – as in vanilla biscuits

Boston baked beans
Oven, grill and micro-wave symbols
Ounces and grammes
Knives are sharp – so please be careful

Marguerite Patten

The Piccolo Cookbook

Illustrated by Eileen Strange
and Anni Axworthy

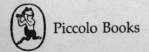 Piccolo Books

This book was originally compiled from *Adventures in Cookery*
(Books 1 and 2), first published 1967 by Ginn & Company Ltd
First published in this form 1971 by Pan Books Ltd,
Cavaye Place, London SW10 9PG
This new extended edition published 1984 by Pan Books Ltd
9 8 7 6 5 4 3
© Marguerite Patten 1967, 1971, additional material 1984
Illustrations © Eileen Strange 1971
Additional illustrations © Anni Axworthy 1984
ISBN 0 330 28540 8
Phototypeset by Input Typesetting Ltd, London
Printed and bound in Great Britain by
Richard Clay (The Chaucer Press) Ltd, Bungay, Suffolk

Contents

bacon and sausages – Sausages for a party –
Hamburgers – Stuffed jacket potatoes – Bird in a nest –
Toppings for jacket potatoes – Cauliflower cheese –
Other ways to use a cheese sauce – Using cooked
vegetables – Macaroni cheese – Toad-in-the-hole –
Golden rules for making a good batter

Introduction

Cooking should be fun, as well as a means of providing enjoyable and interesting dishes for your friends and yourself. The dishes in this book are both varied and easy to cook, and they look and taste good, so you should feel very satisfied when you have prepared them. The contents pages, *v* and *vi*, will show you the range of meals and dishes that are included.

Each recipe in the book tells you exactly how many servings it will make. If you want to make more or less, you simply double or halve the quantities.

Before you start cooking I think it would help if you read pages *viii* to *xiv*, for they tell you about some of the basic foods, like flour, that you will use, and also about some of the 'tools' and equipment found in modern kitchens. Cookery has a special language, so I have also explained some of the words you will find in the recipes.

Just one important warning: please do be careful when you use knives and hot cookers, especially where you have a gas or electric hob set in the working surface and where the outside door of the cooker tends to get hot. See that saucepan handles are turned *in* towards the cooker, and if you do burn your fingers on hot tins, etc., cool them immediately in cold water and let a grown-up know. Do clear up as you work; it makes it easier for you and grown-ups will be more likely to let you do some cooking again if there is no mess.

Good luck, and I hope you like the book.

Marguerite Patten

Some foods you will use

Fats: butter gives a lovely flavour in cooking; bring it out of the refrigerator some little time ahead so it is easier to handle for rubbing in and creaming. There are two basic types of margarine. Hard margarine should be treated like butter. Soft margarine, sometimes called 'luxury' margarine, can be rubbed in or creamed straight from the refrigerator; see pages 125–6.

Flour: plain flour is used for pastry; see page 117. It helps to keep it a good shape. Self-raising flour is ideal for making cakes or scones; see pages 113–15 and 121–31. It has just the right amount of raising agent. If you use plain flour, sieve the quantity of baking powder given in the recipe with the flour. There are various kinds of flour on sale and these are mentioned where suitable. 'Strong flour' is for making bread and other recipes using yeast as well as richer kinds of pastry. 'Soft wheat sponge flour' is for light cakes and sponges; see pages 125 and 126. Wheatmeal and granary flour are mentioned on page 115.

Sugars: caster sugar is used in some recipes to give a better texture. Brown sugar gives a good colour and flavour. If these are not available use granulated sugar.

Some tools you will use

Here are some of the tools mentioned in the recipes:

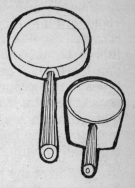

Frying-pans and saucepans: make sure you choose them large enough for the amount of food. If you have non-stick pans ask a grown-up to show you how to take care of them.

Knives: are very important when you cook. *Always be very careful how you use a sharp knife*, which you need for cutting and chopping. Always ask a grown-up to help you chop difficult things. If you have a chopping board, cut on this, so you do not mark the table. Cut bread with a bread knife on a bread or chopping board unless you are using ready-sliced bread. Spread butter on bread with a flat-bladed knife; a pointed knife makes holes in the bread. Lift food out of pans, etc., with a wide-bladed knife called a palette knife, or use a fish slice, that looks like this.

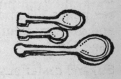

Spoons: when you stir use a wooden spoon; but when you measure use the type of spoon in the recipe. *Always have just enough food to give a level spoon measure. If you overfill the spoon you have too much for the recipe.*

Scales: if you have no scales a grown-up will help you work out the amounts. Today some people use metric measures (grammes and kilos); others use imperial measures (ounces and pounds). This book gives you both; metric measures come first and imperial follow in brackets immediately afterwards, so you can choose which to follow.

Measures: if you have a proper measure use it, but a teacup holds about 142 ml (¹/₄ pint); a breakfast cup about 284 ml (¹/₂ pint). Many recipes give spoon measures. Always fill the spoon so that it is *level*, not more.

A grater: is used for making pieces of cheese, lemon rind, etc., smaller, and if you rub a slice of bread against the coarse side of the grater you can make breadcrumbs. The picture shows the most usual kind.

A colander: is used for straining vegetables.

Sieves: for straining liquids. Use small ones for tea, etc., larger ones where there is more liquid. You also need a sieve to make sure there are no lumps in flour.

A pastry brush: is used for many things, including greasing tins and dishes. Take a very little margarine or fat from the amount in the recipe, warm this and brush over the dish, or rub the unmelted fat over the tin or dish with greaseproof paper.

An egg whisk or **rotary whisk:** is used to whip cream, beat up egg whites, etc.

Cake tins: there are many sorts of cake tins, but for the recipes in this book you will need a baking tray, patty tins, paper cake cases, and a sandwich tin.

Basins and bowls: you will need a nice big mixing bowl (never try to mix a recipe in too small a bowl, it is very difficult!) and some smaller basins for whisking eggs, whipping cream, and so on.

Electrical appliances

There are many special electrical appliances that you may have in your home, such as a blender (often called a liquidizer). You will find this is mentioned on page 27 for making fluffy drinks. This appliance, like a food processor, is useful for preparing many kinds of foods.

An electric mixer saves time and effort when you have to cream or whisk ingredients, but these expensive appliances must be used only with an adult's permission.

Words used in cooking

Mixing

Beating: means mixing the ingredients together with a very brisk movement. A wooden spoon is generally used.

Blending: also means mixing the ingredients together.

Creaming: means beating fat and sugar together until they are soft and fluffy; use a wooden spoon.

Folding: is a turning movement done gently and slowly with a metal spoon, as in the fruit snow (pages 89–90).

Kneading: means mixing the ingredients firmly together with your hands, as in the vanilla biscuits (pages 132–3).

Rubbing in: is a method of mixing fat with flour with the tips of your fingers; you do this in the fruit crumble (pages 102–3) and in scones and rock buns (pages 113–15 and 121–23).

Whisking: is a very brisk movement to whip cream or egg whites and is done by hand or with a rotary whisk.

Cooking

Baking: is the method of cooking food in the oven, such as cakes.

Boiling: is cooking in liquid at boiling point (100°C or 212°F), as you boil the cauliflower on page 69.

Frying: is cooking in fat; do be careful when you do this. See page 8 which tells you about testing the temperature of the fat.

Grilling: is cooking under the grill in a quick heat.

Simmering: is steady cooking in liquid. You should see an occasional bubble on the surface.

Warming: hot food should be served on hot plates or dishes. Heat these on racks on the top of the cooker, in the warming compartment or in the oven, set very low.

Symbols used in this book

This means you will need to light the gas oven or switch on the electric oven. Your mother may prefer to do this for you. If you have a solid-fuel oven ask your mother or a grown-up to explain it.

This symbol is for the grill, and shows that you will need to use it.

This shows that you use the top of the cooker. Ask your mother to explain how to turn down the burner or hotplate during cooking.

This means you need to weigh the food on scales. This book gives both metric weights (grammes and kilos) and imperial weights (oz and lb).

This is the symbol used to show there are directions for using a microwave cooker. This is a very special electrical appliance and it should be used only with permission and under an adult's guidance.

1 Making breakfast

It would be a very nice surprise for the family if you prepared breakfast one morning. Here are three breakfast menus you might try, depending on what sort of breakfast your family likes:

Menu 1
Cornflakes or other breakfast cereal with milk and sugar.
Toast or bread, butter, and marmalade or honey.
Coffee (with cold or hot milk and sugar) (pages 22–3).

Menu 2
Orange juice.
Boiled eggs (pages 9–10).
Toast, butter, marmalade.
Tea (you will need cold milk and sugar on the table) (pages 20–21).

Menu 3
Halved fresh grapefruit or canned grapefruit. Bacon and egg (pages 11–13).
Toast, butter, marmalade.
Tea (you will need cold milk and sugar on the table) (pages 20–21).

Step by step to breakfast

a Decide on your menu.

b Lay the table.

c If you decide on menu 1:

1 Put on the water for the coffee.

2 Put the cereal, etc., on the table.

3 Toast the bread (see below).
Put it on the table with butter and
marmalade or honey.

4 Make the coffee and heat the milk.

How to make toast **when you have
no electric toaster:**

1 Light the gas grill or switch on the
electric grill.

2 Let the grill heat for 1–2 minutes so
that the toast browns quickly without
becoming too hard. You can be
slicing the bread while you are
waiting.

3 Put the slices of bread on the grid
of the grill pan.

4 Watch it as it browns on one side.

5 Turn it over and let it brown on
the other side.

6 When the toast is ready, stand it
up so that it does not become limp
but stays crisp. This is best done in a
toast rack.

d If you decide on menu 2:

1 Halve and squeeze out the
oranges. Pour juice into small
glasses.

2 Toast the bread (see above) and put in a rack on the table with the butter and marmalade

3 Put on the water for cooking the eggs.

4 Boil the kettle for making the tea and put the milk and sugar on the table.

5 Make the tea, carry this carefully to the table.

6 Put in the eggs and time them (see page 10).

e If you decide on menu 3:

1 *Either* cut the grapefruit in halves, separate the pieces of fruit with the tip of a sharp knife, and put sugar on the table, *or* open a can of grapefruit and spoon the segments (pieces) and some juice into bowls or grapefruit glasses.

2 Put the plates for bacon and eggs to warm in a low oven, add 1 extra plate.

3 Toast the bread (see above) and put in a rack on the table with the butter and marmalade.

4 Cook the bacon in a frying-pan or under the grill (see pages 58–9) and keep warm on the extra plate (see page 11).

5 Put on the kettle for tea.

6 Make the tea and carry this carefully to the table, put the milk on the table also.

7 Fry the eggs (see pages 11–12) and lift on to the plates with the bacon; keep warm until you have eaten the grapefruit.

Keeping food warm

As you will see in menu 3, step 2, you keep the bacon warm in the oven set to low (this means 250°F, 120°C or gas mark $\frac{1}{2}$). This is the setting to use to keep food warm.

Never keep eggs warm for too long a time – it makes them hard and unappetizing.

Making overnight preparations

If you are in a hurry in the morning, it is a good idea to do some jobs for breakfast the night before.

a You can lay the table, and put everything ready for making tea or coffee, except the milk which should be kept in the refrigerator.

b You can prepare the grapefruit or orange juice.

Muesli

Home-made muesli is easy to make and is an easy uncooked breakfast dish that is very good for you.

To make muesli for 3 small helpings, mix together 3 tablespoons rolled oats (the kind used to make porridge) with 1–2 tablespoons wheat flakes, 1–2 tablespoons sultanas or seedless raisins and 1–2 tablespoons chopped nuts.

This is the basic mixture that can be prepared the night before.

Serve the muesli with sugar or honey and cold milk or yogurt.

Ways to vary muesli

The home-made muesli recipe can be varied in many ways.

If you prefer you could use some of the ready-prepared packet kinds of muesli instead of the home-made kind.

Add unpeeled and chopped apple(s) to the mixture; do this just before serving as apple turns a horrid brown colour if prepared too soon. All kinds of fresh fruit blend well with muesli.

Mix the muesli with orange juice instead of milk or yogurt.

Add a little desiccated coconut to the mixture.

To make porridge

Porridge is an excellent breakfast dish for cold weather. The easiest way to make it is to use quick–cooking rolled oats. Different makes of rolled oats need slightly different amounts of liquid, so read and follow the instructions on the packet. Choose the kind of liquid you prefer. This can be water, or half water and half milk, or all milk.

To make lovely creamy porridge remember to stir well to blend the rolled oats with the liquid and continue stirring just as recommended on the packet.

Don't forget a pinch of salt when you cook porridge.

Serve porridge with or without honey or sugar (some people prefer it without sugar) and with hot or cold milk.

Laying the table for breakfast

1 Put a tablecloth or mats on the table, add napkins.

2 If you have bacon, or other hot food, you need large knives and forks. If the table is of polished wood, you will need mats to stop the hot plates marking the surface.

3 Lay small plates and knives for toast.

4 Add cups, saucers and teaspoons, sugar, and a jug of cold milk (unless you are heating the milk).

5 Put marmalade and a spoon, and butter, with a knife, on the table.

6 Add the toast-rack, or sliced bread.

7 For grapefruit you need dishes on plates together with spoons, or for fruit juice you need glasses.

8 For boiled eggs you need eggcups on plates, and small spoons, with salt and pepper.

9 Put out a heat-resistant mat or stand for the tea or for coffee *and* hot milk.

When making breakfast

There are many other dishes in this book you can prepare for breakfast – for example, many people like scrambled eggs (pages 50–51), or grilled bacon (page 58), or bacon and sausage (pages 58–9). If you ever visit Norway you may be offered cheese for breakfast. You might try this as a change from eggs and bacon. Poached haddock (page 57) is ideal for breakfast, and cold ham with sliced tomatoes is also good.

When frying bread and eggs you must have the fat hot; so watch it carefully as it melts. When the fat has melted, put a tiny cube of bread in the pan and if it turns golden brown *in about 1 minute* you can cook the slice of bread and the eggs. If it burns, or browns more quickly, allow the fat to *cool* slightly and test again.

When heating milk for coffee or cereals see it does not boil, but have a large spoon ready. If the milk looks like boiling, *stir briskly* to lower the temperature.

How to boil an egg

You will need:
1 egg and water to cover

You will use:
saucepan, basin, tablespoon, eggcup.

1 Light the gas burner or switch on the hotplate.

2 Take a rather small saucepan; you may have a special egg saucepan.

3 Put in enough cold water to cover the egg (or eggs). This generally means that the saucepan is half filled.

4 Put the saucepan on the cooker to boil, but do not let the water boil away.

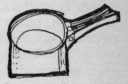

5 Take the egg, in a basin so that it does not fall, and a tablespoon, over to the cooker. Remember that eggs taken straight from the refrigerator or a cold place tend to crack when you put them in boiling water.

6 Put the egg into the spoon, and lower it very gently into the water.

7 Immediately, look at the clock, your watch, or the timer on the cooker (which the instruction card or book will tell you how to set).

8 Some people like to put eggs into cold water, bring to the boil and time from this point. Because the egg starts to cook as the water comes to the boil, the cooking time is shorter.

	Really soft-boiled egg	Firm set egg	Hard-boiled egg
If put in cold water	3 mins	4 mins	10 mins
If put in boiling water	4 mins	5 mins	10 mins

9 Watch the time carefully. Remove the egg from the water with the tablespoon, put into an eggcup and serve immediately.

Hard-boiled eggs

If you are hard-boiling an egg or several eggs to make a salad or special savoury dish as pages 80 and 36, lift the egg(s) from the water, tap the shell(s) sharply and put the egg(s) into cold water. This prevents the egg(s) continuing to cook as they cool down (also see page 36).

Fried bacon and egg

This is one of the nicest breakfast or supper dishes. Read page 8 about frying first.

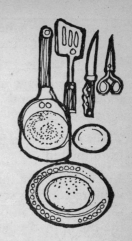

You will need:

bacon	1–2 rashers
egg	1
fat	15 grammes (½ oz)

These ingredients will make 1 serving.

You will use:
sharp knife or kitchen scissors, plate for bacon, frying-pan, fork or tongs, saucer or cup, fish slice, serving plate.

1 Light the gas burner or switch on the electric hotplate.

2 Cut the rinds off the bacon (see note at end of recipe). This makes bacon fat crisp better.

3 If the rashers are very long, cut into halves to fit into the frying-pan.

4 Put the bacon rinds into the frying-pan with the bacon, as they give extra fat for cooking the egg.

5 Cook the bacon until the fat is golden in colour, turning once if the bacon is thick. It usually takes about 3 minutes, but varies with the thickness of the rasher.

6 Lift the bacon on to a warmed plate with a fork or tongs, and remove the rinds from the frying-pan. Keep the bacon hot on the serving plate.

7 Crack the eggshell sharply with a knife or against the edge of a saucer or cup.

8 Pull the halves of the shell apart so that the egg gently drops into the saucer or cup.

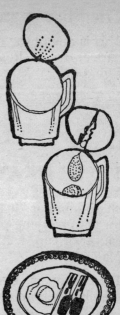

9 Put fat into the frying-pan and heat until melted.

10 Pour the egg into the hot fat. If you are cooking several eggs in the same pan, put in one egg and turn the heat down when the white starts to set. Put in the second egg, and so on.

11 Cook the egg 2 minutes for a lightly set egg or 3 minutes for a firmer egg.

12 Bring the plate with the bacon near the frying-pan.

13 Lift the egg out of the pan with a fish slice and arrange next to the bacon. Serve as soon as possible.

Cleaning a frying-pan

A greasy frying-pan is not very pleasant to wash up so wipe out the pan with newspaper or kitchen paper before washing it. Remember to ask a grown-up how to clean a non-stick frying-pan.

Two ways to cut the rind from bacon

a Lay the rasher of bacon on the chopping board and cut away the rind with a sharp knife.

b Use a pair of kitchen scissors and cut the rind away with these.

Remember to fry rinds to give you extra fat.

Birds love crisp bacon rinds, but they can be used for food for the family too.

To use bacon rinds

Fry the bacon rinds in the frying-pan slowly and steadily until they are very crisp. Turn off the heat and let the rinds become quite cold, then cut them in pieces with kitchen scissors. Use the rinds:

a instead of potato crisps.

b to sprinkle on top of soups and stews.

Bacon and tomato

Another food that goes well with bacon is tomato.

You will need:

bacon	1–2 rashers
tomato	1
salt	pinch
pepper	shake

These ingredients will make 1 serving.

You will use:
kitchen scissors, sharp knife, chopping board, frying-pan, fork or tongs, plate.

1 Cut the rinds off the bacon (see picture, page 13) and cut the tomato in half.

2 Sprinkle the cut sides of tomato with a pinch of salt and a shake of pepper.

3 Put the bacon and bacon rinds, which give extra fat, into the pan. Cook 2 minutes for thin rashers; thicker ones will take longer. The picture shows how you arrange the lean of the second rasher over the fat of the first rasher.

4 When the bacon is nearly cooked, put in the tomato halves and cook for 1 minute. Do not overcook, otherwise tomatoes lose flavour and texture.

5 Lift the bacon and tomato halves on to a hot plate and serve at once.

Two or three *mushrooms* can be fried with bacon instead of the tomato.

Make sure they are not poisonous, if you have picked them – ask a grown-up to look at them.

1 Wash the mushrooms well, and cut the ends off the stalks. If the mushrooms are very good there is no need to skin them.

2 Add a small piece of fat to the frying-pan at stage 3 on page 14.

3 Melt the fat, put in the mushrooms and cook gently for about 5 minutes.

Bacon and apple rings

Apples go well with bacon. A large cooking apple will give enough apple rings for 2 people.

1 Wash the apple in cold water, dry it well and put it on to a chopping board.

2 Press out the core with an apple corer; the picture shows how to do this.

3 Cut the apple into 0.5 cm/¼ inch rings or ask a grown-up to do this for you.

4 Add a small piece of fat to the frying-pan at stage 3 on page 14, melt fat, put in the apple rings and cook gently for about 5 minutes.

Bacon and fried bread

Crisp fried bread makes a breakfast or supper more satisfying. Make sure the fat is really hot at stage 2 so the bread browns well.

You will need:

bacon	1–2 rashers
bread	small slice

These ingredients will make 1 serving.

You will use:
sharp knife or kitchen scissors, frying-pan, fork or tongs, plate, bread knife and board, fish slice.

1 Cook the bacon and bacon rinds as fried bacon and egg to stage 4.

2 Lift the bacon on to a hot plate.

3 Make sure the fat in the pan is really hot (see page 8). Put the slice of bread into the frying-pan and cook for 1 minute. Then turn it and cook for another minute until crisp and brown.

Using a microwave cooker for bacon

You can cook bacon in a microwave cooker. Prepare the bacon, then ask a grown-up to show you how to use the microwave. Tomatoes and mushrooms can be cooked this way too, but it is not possible to make fried bread.

Breakfast in bed

You may like to give your mother or father breakfast in bed for a special treat, perhaps on their birthdays, or you may have someone at home who is ill and needs breakfast in bed. You can serve the same kind of menus as on page 1, but remember you have to carry the tray so do not make it too heavy or try to prepare anything too complicated.

1 Put on a cloth to make the tray look pretty, add a napkin and plate, cup, etc.

2 If it is a special day, like a birthday, perhaps you could put a small flower into a tiny vase or eggcup.

3 Make the toast and put it on the tray, either in a small rack or on a plate, with tiny dishes of butter and marmalade.

4 Prepare orange juice or grapefruit or cereal.

5 Make the tea or coffee. Pour out a cup of tea or coffee, add milk, put on the tray with sugar if wished. *Do not* try to carry up a tea, or coffee, pot.

6 Have a final check that everything is on the tray and carry it slowly and carefully to the bedroom.

7 Once you have left the person in bed comfortably eating their breakfast, don't forget to return after five or ten minutes to refill their cup and offer some more toast.

8 When the person has finished breakfast carry the tray of china and cutlery carefully out of the bedroom.

9 After you have cleared away all the food go back and make sure there are no crumbs left in the bed; brush these away if there are. It is very uncomfortable to try and rest on prickly crumbs!

If a person is unwell or just resting they will be pleased to have a nice cold drink left beside the bed. Fill a jug with cold water or fruit juice or home-made lemonade. There is an easy recipe on page 30. Put a glass beside the jug.

2 Making drinks

In this section you will find tea, coffee, milk shakes and other interesting drinks. Most recipes mention 'cups' – these are teacups.

Remember:

If you are boiling water in a kettle, make sure the lid is firm so it cannot fall off as you pour out the boiling water. Do not fill the kettle more than three-quarters full.

Hold the kettle firmly. Pour carefully, with spout away from you, so the steam cannot scald you.

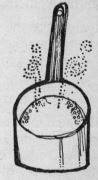

Do not allow milk to *boil*, for this causes a skin; just heat the milk until it bubbles round the edge – this is called *simmering*. Other recipes talk about *simmering* when the liquid only bubbles gently.

Fill a 'milky' saucepan with cold water after using it; this makes it easier to wash up.

When you fill a glass tumbler with a hot drink, pour slowly and keep a spoon in the glass. This helps to prevent it cracking.

How to make tea

The most important thing to remember is to take the teapot to the kettle, and not the kettle to the teapot. In this way you will be sure of pouring really boiling water on to the tea in the pot.

You will need:
tea, *water*, *milk*, *sugar*.

You will use:
kettle, teapot, spoon, jug, cups, saucers and teaspoons.

1 Put water drawn from the *cold* tap into the kettle and put it on to heat.

2 Heat teapot with a little hot water from the kettle.

3 Just before the water in the kettle is boiling, pour the water out of the teapot and put in the tea.

4 For one person only, put in 2 *level* teaspoons of tea.

5 We generally say '1 level teaspoon per person and 1 for the pot', so for four people put in 5 *level* teaspoons of tea for a really strong brew. For a weak tea use a little less.

6 The moment the water in the kettle boils, turn or switch off the heat. With an electric kettle, pull out the plug after switching off the heat.

7 Hold the kettle firmly; then pour the boiling water steadily over the tea.

8 Put the lid on the teapot and let it stand for several minutes. Some people stir the tea first, then let it stand.

9 Pour the cold milk into the jug, then pour a little cold milk into each cup from the jug; everyone helps themselves to sugar if they like it.

10 When the leaves fall to the bottom of the pot the tea is ready to be poured. You can use a tea strainer if you wish.

Using tea bags

Nowadays tea bags have become very popular. They are an easy way of making tea. Use one tea bag per person.

Warm the pot as stages 1 and 2 on page 20, then put the tea bags into the heated teapot and continue as stages 7 to 9 on this page.

You can put a tea bag into a teacup, add boiling water, allow the tea to stand for 2–3 minutes then lift the tea bag out of the cup; add cold milk and sugar to taste.

How to make coffee

There are a number of ways to make coffee. You may have a percolator or other coffee-maker at home, but making it in a jug is a good, as well as easy, way.

You will need:
ground coffee, water, milk, sugar.

You will use:
kettle, tablespoon, jug, coffee strainer, saucepan, cups and saucers.

1 Put water, drawn from the cold water tap, on to boil.

2 For 1 cup of coffee: allow $\frac{1}{8}$ litre (125 ml) or $\frac{1}{4}$ pint water, so work out how much water to heat according to the number of cups of coffee you want. For example, for 4 cups of coffee you will need 1 pint or $\frac{1}{2}$ litre of water.

3 Allow about $\frac{1}{2}$ teacup of milk for each person.

4 To $\frac{1}{2}$ litre (500 ml) or 1 pint water use 2 rounded tablespoons (or 4 level tablespoons) of ground coffee.

5 Warm the jug for coffee (as for tea, see page 20). Put in the coffee.

6 Pour on the boiling water and let it stand for 1 minute; then stir with a spoon.

7 Put a lid on the coffee jug or use a folded teacloth. Let the coffee stand for 5 minutes in a warm place.

8 Meanwhile heat the milk; do not let it boil, for this spoils the flavour of coffee and the milk forms a skin which most people dislike. Some people prefer cold milk in coffee.

9 When the coffee is ready, pour it, through a strainer if you have one, into cups or into a warm coffee pot.

10 If you have no strainer, pour carefully, for although most of the coffee grounds sink to the bottom, some may rise if you pour too rapidly.

11 Add hot milk to each cup, or pour it into a separate jug and serve immediately.

Using instant coffee

You may find it quicker and easier to use instant coffee powder.

Measure out a teaspoon of the coffee powder into a cup.

Blend this with very hot water, then add hot or cold milk and sugar to taste.

Drinks with milk

Milk gives lots of interesting drinks for children and grown-ups. The recipes on the next pages show how to make milky drinks of all kinds.

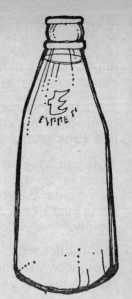

And of course milk is very nice served hot or cold without any flavourings at all.

At bedtime it is a good idea to flavour hot or cold milk with Horlicks or Ovaltine or one of the other malt flavourings.

Read the instructions on the tin and follow them carefully.

You will need to measure the milk in a measuring jug or in the cup or glass you are going to use before making the drinks so no milk is wasted.

Iced coffee

This is an excellent way of having cold coffee and milk.

Make the coffee with ground or instant coffee. Let this become cold and chill it in the refrigerator.

Put an ice cube into a tall glass then half fill the glass with the very cold coffee.

Fill the glass with cold milk.

Cold mocha drink

A mixture of coffee and chocolate flavours is often given the name of 'mocha'. You can make a delicious light cold drink in a blender (liquidizer).

1 Put half a cup of cold milk and half a cup of cold coffee into the goblet of the blender.

2 Add 1–2 teaspoons of chocolate powder and 1–2 teaspoons of sugar, if you like sweet drinks.

3 Put the lid on the blender goblet and place this in position.

4 Switch on the blender and leave it running for about 25–30 seconds or until you have made a fluffy drink.

5 Pour this into a tall glass.

Note! If you have no blender follow the directions on page 27 for making the chocolate milk shake.

Hot chocolate

You will need:

milk	1 cup
chocolate powder	2–3 teaspoons

These ingredients will make 1 cup.

You will use:
cup and saucer, saucepan, teaspoon.

1 Heat the milk in a saucepan.

2 Stir in chocolate and pour into a cup. Hot chocolate whisked with a fork or a whisk before it is poured into the cup is frothy and more delicious.

Cocoa

You will need:

milk (or use half milk and half water)	1 cup
cocoa	1 teaspoon
sugar	to taste

These ingredients will make 1 cup.

You will use:
cup and saucer, teaspoon, tablespoon, saucepan.

1 Put the cocoa into a cup, stir in 2 tablespoons of cold milk, blend until smooth.

2 Heat the rest of the milk, pour over the cocoa; add sugar.

Some people like to pour the cocoa mixture back into the pan and heat it for 1 minute, then return it to the cup.

Hot mocha drink

Make the drink with chocolate or cocoa as in the recipe on page 25 or on this page, but use half coffee and half milk instead of all milk.

Chocolate milk shake

You will need:

milk	1 glass
chocolate powder	2 teaspoons

These ingredients will make 1 glass.

You will use:
teaspoon, bowl, egg whisk, glass.

1 Measure a glassful of milk into the bowl.

2 Whisk in the chocolate powder until it is fully dissolved and the milk looks fluffy.

3 Pour into a clean glass.

You can serve with straws, and add a spoonful of ice-cream for special occasions, or cream and grated chocolate. Chocolate powder is sweetened so no sugar is needed.

Using a blender

You can use a blender (liquidizer) for mixing this and all other milk shakes.

Rose hip milk shake

This is a milk shake that gives you the Vitamin C from rose hip syrup as well as the food value of milk. The milk should be really cold.

You will need:

milk	³/₄ glass
rose hip syrup	1 or 2 tablespoons

These ingredients will make 1 glass.

You will use:
basin, tablespoon, egg whisk, glass.

1 Pour the milk into a basin.

2 Add the rose hip syrup.

3 Whisk together with an egg whisk and pour into the glass.

Yogurt drinks

If you enjoy yogurt you can make delicious drinks using it.

Choose a fruit-flavoured yogurt and whisk it with enough cold milk to make a pouring mixture. You can make the drinks in a blender (liquidizer), or as on page 29.

More milk shakes

The chocolate and rose hip syrup milk shakes show you how to make a milk shake in a basin. There are many ways of flavouring milk.

a Whisk the cold milk with a tablespoon of flavoured ice-cream.

b Use a special sweetened syrup and whisk a tablespoon of this with the cold milk.

c Use blackcurrant syrup instead of rose hip syrup.

d You can use a little mashed fresh fruit with the cold milk; whisk a small mashed banana with a teaspoon of sugar and $3/4$ of a glass of cold milk.

e Whisk 2 tablespoons mashed fresh raspberries and a little sugar with $3/4$ of a glass of cold milk.

To get a very fluffy milk shake, as served in a milk bar, put the ingredients into a fairly tall jug and whisk hard with a flat or rotary beater. If you can use an electric liquidizer or blender, you will get an even better result.

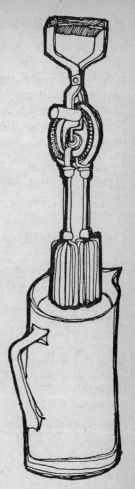

Quick lemonade

This is very easy to make. Hot lemonade is very good if you have a cold. Be careful the water is not too hot as it will crack the glass; stand a spoon in the glass (see page 19). You can sweeten with honey instead of sugar.

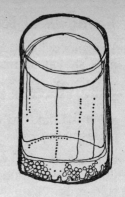

You will need:

lemon	1
sugar	2 teaspoons
water	to taste

These ingredients will make 1 glass.

You will use:
knife, lemon squeezer, teaspoon, glass.

1 Cut the lemon in halves and squeeze out the juice.

2 Put the juice with the sugar into a glass and add hot or cold water.

Quick orangeade

Oranges have a less strong flavour than lemons, so you will need about half a tumbler of freshly squeezed orange juice or orange juice from a can, carton or bottle to give a good flavour.

Economical lemonade

You use the flavour from the lemon peel as well as from the juice.

You will need:

lemons	2 large
sugar	1–2 tablespoons
boiling water	⁵/₈ litre (625 ml) or 1¹/₄ pints

These ingredients will make 4 glasses.

You will use:
knife, lemon squeezer, 3 jugs (make sure one of these is safe for boiling water), kettle, tablespoon, strainer.

1 Halve the lemons and squeeze out the juice, put this into the smallest jug.

2 Put the lemon halves into a large jug which has previously been warmed; add sugar. Pour over the boiling water.

3 Let this water cool and, as it cools, press the lemon halves hard to get out as much flavour as possible.

4 Strain into the clean jug and add the lemon juice.

You can use 3–4 large oranges instead of 2 large lemons.

Fruit cup

A special drink for a party.

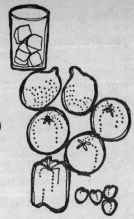

You will need:

lemons	2
oranges	2
water	1 cup
sugar	50 grammes (2 oz)
pineapple juice	1 can
ice cubes	few
soda water	½ litre/500 ml (1 pint)

to decorate:

orange	1
apple	1
glacé cherries	few

These ingredients will make 8–10 glasses.

You will use:
potato peeler or sharp knife, cup, saucepan, strainer, basin, wooden spoon, lemon squeezer, can opener, large bowl for serving.

1 Cut away the peel from the fruit used in the drink (*not* in the decoration), and put this in the saucepan and simmer with the water for 5 minutes. (It is very easy to peel fruit with a potato peeler, if you have one.)

2 Strain the hot liquid over the sugar which is in a basin.

3 Stir until the sugar has dissolved, then cool.

4 Squeeze the juice from the lemons and oranges, open the can of pineapple juice.

5 Put some ice cubes into the serving bowl, add the fruit juices and the sugar mixture.

6 Just before serving, add the soda water and decorate with the thinly sliced fruit and cherries.

More fruit cups

Now you have made one kind of fruit cup, try others.

Apple fruit cup. Use apple juice instead of pineapple.

Cider cup. Use sweet cider instead of pineapple juice. You can buy non-alcoholic cider as well as the alcoholic kind.

Ginger fruit cup. Use ginger ale or ginger beer; omit soda water.

Note! You may have one of the special appliances for making drinks so you can make your own ginger ale, ginger beer or soda water.

3 Making sandwiches

When you make sandwiches:

1 Spread the thinly cut slices of
bread with butter or margarine and
add the filling to half the slices of
bread. If you intend to make very
dainty sandwiches and cut the crusts
off the bread, do not take the filling
to the very edges.

2 Cover with the other slices of bread
and butter.

3 Put the sandwich on to a chopping
board or bread board, remove the
crusts if you wish.

4 Cut the whole sandwich into 2 or 4
triangles or squares.

You may prefer to cut the
sandwiches into fingers.

On the next page are some
suggestions for *sandwich fillings*, but
you will be able to think up many
others.

Some sandwich fillings

Cheese. Either put slices of cheese or grated cheese on the bread and butter, or spread cream cheese over the bread and butter; add lettuce or sliced tomato or a little chutney, if wished.

Egg. You can either hard-boil the eggs and slice them with a knife or egg slicer, or you can make an egg into a more interesting filling (see next page). Lettuce or sprigs of watercress or mustard and cress go well with egg.

Ham. Use thin slices of cooked ham. You can add lettuce or sliced tomato.

Sardine. Open a can of sardines (if you find this difficult, ask a grown-up to help you), put the fish into a basin and mash, added a pinch of salt and a shake of pepper

Tomatoes. Slice the tomatoes, put them on bread and butter, add a pinch of salt and a shake of pepper. Add lettuce or sliced cucumber if wished. Some people like a drop of vinegar in tomato sandwiches.

Banana and honey. For a delicious, sweet sandwich, spread bread and butter with honey, and add some slices of banana.

Egg sandwiches

You will need:

thin slices of bread 2 large or 4 small
butter or margarine 25 grammes (1 oz)

for the filling:
eggs 2
butter or margarine 25 grammes (1 oz)
salt pinch
pepper shake

These ingredients will make 2 servings.

You will use:
saucepan, tablespoon, basin, sharp
knife, fork, saucer or plate for butter,
bread knife, bread board, flat-bladed
knife, plate.

1 Hard-boil the eggs for the time
given in the table (see page 10).

2 As soon as they are cooked, lift out
of the water and tap the shells. (This
lets the steam out and prevents an
ugly dark ring forming round the
yolk.)

3 Put into a basin of cold water.
Allow the eggs to get quite cold.

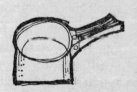

4 Remove the shells, put the eggs
into a basin and cut them into small
pieces with the knife and fork.

5 Add the butter or margarine, a
pinch of salt and a shake of pepper.

6 Mash everything together with a
fork. The mixture is then ready to
spread on bread or bread and butter.

7 Spread the bread with the butter.

8 Spread half the slices of bread with the egg mixture, then cover with the other slices of bread and butter.

9 Cut away the crusts if wished, then cut the sandwiches into fingers or triangles.

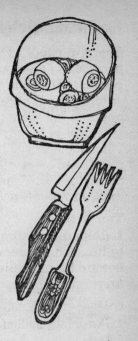

You can spread the bread with potted meat or fish paste at stage 7, then add the egg mixture.

To make a change

Hard-boiled eggs blend well with many different foods, for example you could make:

Egg and cheese sandwiches. Add 50 grammes (2 oz) of cream cheese or grated cheese to the egg mixture at stage 6.

Egg and ham sandwiches. Cut 25–50 grammes (1–2 oz) of cooked ham into small pieces with a knife. Add to the egg mixture at stage 6.

Egg and watercress sandwiches. Wash and dry several sprigs of watercress, pull off the leaves and cut these into small pieces with kitchen scissors. Add to the egg mixture at stage 6.

Open sandwiches

In Scandinavia – Denmark, in
particular – open sandwiches are very
popular. The filling is not covered
with a second slice of bread, but lies
open on one slice of bread. Choose
any kind of bread: white, brown,
wholemeal or rye bread or
crispbread. Spread the bread with
plenty of butter, and arrange the
food on top. Here are some ideas for
fillings:

1 Roll up thin slices of cooked ham
or luncheon meat, arrange on the
buttered bread, and top with a little
mayonnaise or cream cheese and
parsley or a slice of orange.

2 Put a lettuce leaf on the buttered
bread, then add sliced cheese and
halved grapes; take out the grape
pips before putting on to the cheese.

3 Put a lettuce leaf on the buttered
bread, then add rings of hard-boiled
egg and sliced tomato.

Open sandwiches make a good snack
if you have a few friends visiting
you.

You can eat small open sandwiches
with your fingers, but large open
sandwiches should be served with a
knife and fork.

Toasted cheese club sandwich

You will need:

white or brown	
bread	3 slices
thinly sliced	25–50 grammes
Cheddar cheese	(1–2 oz)
made mustard	a little
thinly sliced tomato	1
grilled bacon	1–2 rashers
lettuce leaf	1
salad cream or	
mayonnaise	a little

These ingredients will make 1–2 servings.

You will use:
plate, sharp knife, chopping board.
flat-bladed knife, teaspoon.

1 Switch on or light the grill.

2 Toast the bread on both sides; grill the bacon.

3 Cover one slice of toast with the cheese and a little mustard, and the thinly sliced tomato.

4 Lay the second slice of toast on top, and then the grilled bacon.

5 Top with a lettuce leaf and a little salad cream or mayonnaise and the third slice of toast.

6 Cut across, and serve at once.

There are many varieties of toasted sandwiches, for example:

a Sliced ham and sliced cheese.

b Mashed sardines and chopped hard-boiled egg.

c Flaked canned salmon and chopped gherkin.

d Fried bacon and fried egg.

Preparations to make ahead:
Cut the rind off the bacon with kitchen scissors or a knife.

Slice the bread (unless using sliced bread), the cheese and tomato.

Wash the lettuce (see page 77).

Using a sandwich toaster

You may have an electric sandwich toaster in your kitchen. Make the sandwiches following the suggestions on this page and page 39, but instead of toasting the bread, ask a grown-up to show you how to use the sandwich toaster and cook the sandwiches in the heated toaster.

4 Making quick snacks

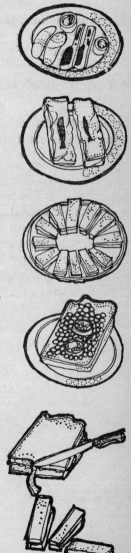

There are many kinds of quick and easy snacks, and you can serve these for supper or for tea.

I hope you enjoy the recipes here. They show you how to make snacks that are served on toast and others that are rather more substantial.

If you plan to serve the snacks on trays, lay the trays *before* you start cooking the food; cut toasted snacks into fingers so they are easier to manage.

If you prefer to eat them sitting at the table, then the section on pages 111 and 112 will help you lay the table so you do not forget anything.

When making snacks, remember:

1 Put the plates to warm first, in a warming drawer or very low oven.

2 Do not try and do too many things at one time; for example, when making a toasted snack watch the toast and then do the topping. You can put the buttered toast on the warm plates until you are ready to add the other ingredients.

3 Serve the snacks as soon as they
are made.

Easy snacks

Mushrooms on toast. Prepare then
fry mushrooms in a little fat as stages
1–3 on page 15. Spread hot toast with
a little butter or margarine then
spoon the mushrooms on to the
toast.

Spaghetti with cheese. Heat canned
spaghetti as the instructions on the
can. Grate a little cheese. Serve the
spaghetti on heated plates and
sprinkle with the grated cheese.

Tomatoes on toast. Cut tomatoes in
halves; put on the grill pan and cook
for 3–4 minutes under a hot grill.
Spread hot toast with a little butter or
margarine and *carefully* lift the cooked
tomatoes on to the toast.

Cheese on toast

You will need:

bread   1 slice
butter or margarine   15 grammes (¹/₂ oz)
Cheddar or processed
cheese   1 slice

These ingredients will make 1 serving.

You will use:

bread knife, bread board, flat-bladed knife, knife for cutting cheese, serving plate.

1 Switch on or light the grill.

2 Toast the bread on both sides and spread with butter on one side, then cover the buttered side with cheese; put under the hot grill until the cheese begins to melt and bubble. This takes 2–3 minutes.

3 *Do not overcook*, otherwise the cheese becomes tough. The crusts can be cut from the bread, but if left on you have a more substantial meal.

Welsh rarebit

You will need:

butter	15 grammes (½ oz)
grated cheese	50 grammes (2 oz)
made mustard	¼ level teaspoon
salt	pinch
pepper	shake
milk	½ tablespoon
bread for toast	1 slice

to garnish:
parsley or watercress sprig

These ingredients will make 1 serving.

You will use:
basin, wooden spoon, grater, plate, teaspoon, tablespoon, bread knife, bread board, flat-bladed knife, serving plate.

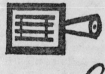

1 Switch on or light the grill.

2 Put the butter into a basin, cream until soft with a wooden spoon, then add rest of ingredients (except the parsley or watercress) and stir thoroughly.

3 Toast the bread, remove the crusts if you wish, spread with the rarebit mixture.

4 Put on to the grill pan and cook under the grill for 3–4 minutes, until brown.

Serve at once, garnished with parsley or watercress.

Now you have made a Welsh rarebit you may like to make more exciting cheese snacks.

Tomato Welsh rarebit

You will need:
Ingredients as Welsh rarebit plus 1 tomato.

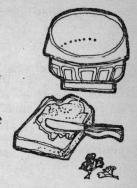

1 Make the cheese mixture as above.

2 Toast and butter the bread.

3 Slice the tomato, then put it on the toast and cover with the cheese mixture.

4 Cook as before.

Yorkshire rarebit

You will need:
Ingredients as Welsh rarebit plus 1 slice of ham.

1 Make the cheese mixture as before.

2 Toast the bread, butter it, then top with the ham slice.

3 Cover with the rarebit mixture and cook as before.

Sardine rarebit

You will need:
Ingredients as Welsh rarebit plus 2 sardines.

1 Make the cheese mixture as before, and the toast.

2 Cook the rarebit mixture until brown, top with the sardines and heat for 1 minute only.

3 Cut into 2 fingers – see picture.

Beans on toast

This is very easy and well known. It makes a tasty snack and is a good protein food and an excellent source of fibre.

You will need:

beans in tomato sauce	1 small can
bread	1 slice
butter or margarine	15 grammes (½ oz)

These ingredients will make 1 or 2 small servings.

You will use:
can opener, saucepan, bread knife, bread board, flat-bladed knife, plate.

1 Switch on or light the grill.

2 Heat beans as directed on can. *Do not overcook*, as the beans will break and become mushy. The flavour is improved if you add a knob of butter and a *little* pepper to the beans as they cook.

3 Toast bread on both sides; spread with butter on one side.

4 Put toast on the plate and pile the hot beans on top. Soak the saucepan in cold water immediately.

To make beans on toast more exciting, you can serve them with a rasher of grilled bacon and a tomato halved and grilled.

Ways to use baked beans

We generally call beans in tomato sauce 'baked beans'. They can be used in many ways.

Baked bean sandwiches. Open a can of baked beans, tip them into a basin and mash well. Grate a little cheese, mix with the beans. Use as filling in ordinary or toasted sandwiches.

Bean chowder. Open a small can of tomato soup and a small can of baked beans. Tip the soup and the beans into a saucepan and heat them together. 'Chowder' is an American word for a thick soup. You can add little pieces of chopped cooked ham or bacon to the chowder.

Sweet and sour baked beans. Open a small can of baked beans and tip into a basin. Add a good tablespoon of chutney (if the chutney has large pieces in it you will need to cut these up before adding to the baked beans).

Stir in a few drops of vinegar or lemon juice to give a slightly sharp flavour.

Speedy Boston baked beans

The true American recipe takes many hours to prepare and cook, for it is made with dried haricot beans. You can prepare a very good speedy recipe as follows:

1 Buy a piece of salt fat pork weighing about 175 grammes (6 oz) from the butcher. If you cannot get this use a thick rasher of streaky bacon instead.

2 Cut the pork or bacon into pieces; do not discard the rind as this can be chopped and used to give flavour.

3 Peel and chop 1 medium-sized onion.

4 Open a large can of beans in tomato sauce and tip these into a large basin; add the pieces of pork or bacon and the onion.

5 Stir in $\frac{1}{2}$ teaspoon dry mustard powder, $\frac{1}{2}$–1 level tablespoon brown sugar, 1 level tablespoon black treacle, a pinch of salt and pepper and 4 tablespoons of water.

6 Mix all the ingredients together then spoon into an ovenproof casserole. Cover the casserole very well.

7 Cook in a slow oven (300°F, 150°C or gas mark 2) for $1\frac{1}{2}$ hours. Serve hot or cold.

Scrambled egg

You will need:

bread	1 slice
butter or margarine	15 grammes ($\frac{1}{2}$ oz)
eggs	1 or 2
salt	pinch
pepper	shake
milk	1 dessertspoon

to garnish:
parsley   small sprig

These ingredients will make 1 serving.

You will use:
bread knife, bread board, flat-bladed knife, serving plate, basin, fork, saucepan, wooden spoon.

1 Switch on or light the grill.

2 Toast and butter the bread. Keep warm on a plate in the warming drawer or a very low oven while cooking the eggs.

3 Break the egg or eggs into a basin, add salt, pepper and milk, and beat with a fork.

4 Melt a little butter in a saucepan. Add the egg and milk. Turn heat very low and cook slowly.

5 Stir with a wooden spoon, moving the egg from the bottom of the pan all the time, until the mixture begins to thicken.

6 Remove pan from heat, for the egg continues to cook in the hot saucepan. *Never allow scrambled egg to get too set.*

7 Pile on to hot buttered toast, put the parsley on top. Serve at once.

It is easier to wash the saucepan if you put it to soak at once in cold water. One egg makes a small portion suitable for breakfast. For a more generous helping, use 2 eggs.

Using a microwave cooker for scrambled egg

It is not possible to boil eggs in a microwave cooker but scrambled eggs are *very* satisfactory.

Make the toast as stages 1 and 2 on page 50 and prepare the egg or eggs as stage 3 on page 50.

Put the butter into an ovenproof dish – you cannot use metal saucepans in a microwave cooker. Melt the butter in the microwave cooker; an adult will show you how to do this.

Add the egg(s) to the hot butter and cook in the microwave; you will need to switch off and stir the egg(s) once or twice. Serve as stage 7.

Making an omelette

An omelette is not easy to make, so it is a good idea to watch an adult make one on several occasions.

You will need:

eggs	2
salt	pinch
pepper	shake
water	1 tablespoon
butter	15–25 grammes (¹/₂–1 oz)

These ingredients will make 1 serving.

You will use:
basin, cup, fork, tablespoon, small omelette pan, flat-bladed knife, fish slice (optional), serving plate.

1 Break the first egg into a basin. Break the second egg into the cup to make sure it is fresh, transfer it to the basin, add the salt, pepper and water, and beat with a fork until the eggs are mixed.

2 Light the gas burner or switch on the electric hotplate to moderately hot. Use the smaller amount of butter with a non-stick pan, but the larger amount with an ordinary pan (this needs more fat). Butter is the best fat for cooking an omelette; heat until melted.

3 Pour the eggs into the hot butter. Do not stir the eggs in the pan. Leave them cooking for about 30 seconds, to form a thin cooked layer.

4 At the end of this time hold the handle of the pan firmly with your left hand and tilt the pan *very slightly*; this allows the uncooked egg to run towards the edges of the pan.

5 While this is happening, hold the knife in your right hand and loosen the omelette away from the sides of the pan. The process given in stages 4 and 5 is known as 'working' the omelette.

6 When the eggs are set, slip the flat-bladed knife under the omelette and fold it away from the handle of the omelette pan.

7 Either slip the fish slice under the omelette and lift it out of the pan or slide the omelette from the pan on to the serving plate.

Ways to flavour an omelette

a Add a tablespoon of chopped parsley to the eggs at stage 3, page 52.

b Add 25 grammes (1 oz) of grated cheese at stage 6 before folding the omelette.

c Add 25 grammes (1 oz) of chopped ham to the eggs at stage 3, page 52.

Cheese dreams

A quick and delicious supper dish of fried sandwiches. Use ready-sliced bread if possible so the slices are an even thickness.

You will need:

bread	8 slices
butter	75–100 grammes (3–4 oz)
cheese	50–75 grammes (2–3 oz)
fat for frying	50 grammes (2 oz)

These ingredients will make about 4 good servings.

You will use:
flat-bladed knife, bread board for bread and butter, grater, plate, sharp knife, frying-pan, fish slice, serving dish.

1 You will use the gas boiling ring or electric hotplate.

2 Spread the bread with the butter, keep on the board.

3 Grate the cheese on to a plate.

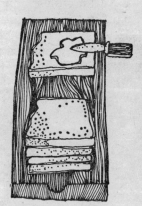

4 Cover half the slices of bread and butter with the grated cheese.

5 Put the rest of the slices of bread and butter over the cheese to make sandwiches.

6 Cut the sandwiches into neat fingers. There is no need to cut off the crusts.

7 Heat the fat in the frying-pan but be very careful it does not become too hot. Fry until the sandwiches are crisp and golden brown on the underside.

8 Turn carefully with a fish slice and fry on the second side.

9 Lift out on to a hot serving dish and eat at once.

Buying cheese

Cheese is an important protein food. Uncooked cheese can make an excellent main dish. Serve the cheese with salad as on page 81 or in sandwiches or with crusty rolls or bread and an apple or tomato. When you go shopping you will find a great variety of cheese from which to choose. Try some of the varieties you have not tasted before. Cheddar, Cheshire, Double Gloucester, Edam, Gouda or Gruyère are excellent cooking cheeses.

Sardines on toast

Canned sardines make good supper
dishes and are nice in salads. Ask a
grown-up to open the can with the
special key.

You will need:

bread	1 slice
butter or margarine	15 grammes (1/2 oz)
sardines	2–3
parsley	sprig

These ingredients will make 1 serving

You will use:
bread knife, bread board, flat-bladed
knife, fork, basin (see stage 3), plate.

1 Switch on or light the grill.

2 Toast the bread on both sides;
butter on one side.

3 Either put sardines whole on the
toast, or mash them in a basin first,
then spread over the toast.

4 Put the toast back under a hot grill
for 2 minutes and arrange parsley on
top before serving.

Poached haddock

This smoked yellow fish is good for breakfast or supper.

You will need:

smoked haddock   1 medium fillet
water   about ¹/₂ litre
                   (1 pint)
butter or margarine 2 small pieces

These ingredients will make 2 servings.

You will use:
kitchen scissors or knife, chopping board, bowl, kitchen paper, measuring jug, large saucepan, fish slice, serving dish.

1 Cut the fish in 2 pieces, wash in cold water, dry on kitchen paper.

2 Put the water and fish into the saucepan and bring the water to the boil; turn down the heat, simmer gently for 5 minutes until the fish is tender.

3 Lift the fish out of the liquid with a fish slice and place on previously warmed dish.

4 Serve with pieces of margarine or butter on top.

Grilled bacon and sausages

Grilling makes food less fatty than frying, and is just as quick and easy.

You will need:

sausages	1–2
bacon	1–2 rashers
tomato	1
made mustard for serving (optional)	

These ingredients will make 1 serving.

You will use:
fork, sharp knife, chopping board, plate, tongs.

1 Switch on or light the grill.

2 Prick the sausages, put on the grid of grill pan and put under the hot grill.

3 Cook for 8–10 minutes, turning, so they brown evenly all over. Add rasher of bacon with the rind cut off and tomato halves, and finish cooking. Turn the bacon once if thick, but there is no need to turn the tomatoes.

4 Serve with mustard if wished.

When grilling a lot of bacon and sausages you may not have room for both in the pan, so cook the sausages first, put on a hot dish and keep warm. Then cook the bacon and tomatoes.

Fried bacon and sausages

Fried bacon and sausages make a quick supper dish. If you would rather grill than fry them, see the previous recipe.

You will need:

sausages	1 or 2
bacon	1–2 rashers

made mustard for serving (optional)

These ingredients will make 1 serving.

You will use:
fork, frying-pan, plate for keeping sausages warm, serving plate, tongs.

1 Light the gas burner or switch on the electric hotplate. Put plates to warm in very low oven or warming drawer.

2 As sausages take longer to cook than bacon, these are fried first.

3 Prick each sausage with a fork to stop the skins splitting.

4 Put into the frying-pan without fat.

5 Cook slowly, turning the sausages as they brown. Large sausages will take about 15 minutes, chipolata sausages will take about 10 minutes.

6 When the sausages are cooked, put them on to a hot plate.

7 Prepare and cook the bacon (see pages 11–12) and serve with the sausages. Most people like mustard with sausages. You can make this up from powder or use made mustard.

Kinds of sausages

Sausages are usually made from pork, but you can buy beef sausages too. There are many types:

a Sausages from the butcher or grocer with skins.

b Sausages without skins. Sometimes these are frozen and you do not need to let them thaw out before you cook them.

c Smaller sausages that are called chipolatas.

d Frankfurter sausages which you can buy in tins or packets or from grocers. These are ready-cooked and just need heating in hot, *but not boiling*, water.

Sausages for a party

Grilled or fried sausages make an excellent party dish. Buy small chipolata or cocktail sausages.

1 Grill or fry the sausages as directed on pages 58 to 60.

2 Press cocktail sticks into the cooked sausages and serve them hot or cold.

3 It makes a more interesting dish if the sausages are served with a dip.

To make a dip to go with 450 grammes (1 lb) of sausages, mix together 4 tablespoons of tomato ketchup and 3 teaspoons of made mustard, put this into a small bowl and place on the dish, as shown in the picture.

Note! Made mustard means either mustard powder mixed with water, or ready-prepared mustard.

Hamburgers

Although these are made with beef they are generally called hamburgers, because it is believed that they were first made in Hamburg in Germany. They can be called 'beefburgers' too. You can buy them frozen or from some butchers but it is easy to make these meat cakes.

You will need:

raw minced best quality stewing steak	225 grammes (8 oz)
salt	pinch
pepper	shake
fat for frying	25 grammes (1 oz)
flavourings	see note

These ingredients will make 2 servings.

Note! You may wish to use garlic, as suggested below. The picture shows a head of garlic; a clove is just one segment. Peel a clove, put a little salt on a chopping board, slice the garlic clove, then crush it with a firm knife.

You will use:
basin, fork, chopping board, frying-pan, fish slice, serving plates.

1 Put the steak into the basin, add the salt and pepper and mix well with the fork. There are many ways of flavouring hamburgers; grated cheese, crushed garlic, Worcestershire sauce, mustard or chopped onion all make delicious additions.

2 Make the mixture into two rounds (like the burgers you buy) on the chopping board with your fingers. Put them into the refrigerator until you are ready to cook and serve (see the suggestions below). Warm the serving plates.

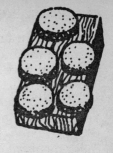

3 Heat the fat in the frying-pan and fry the hamburgers for 2 minutes on one side, turn over with the fish slice and fry on the second side for the same time. They are then ready to serve on the heated plates.

Ways to serve hamburgers

Serve them with vegetables for a main course.

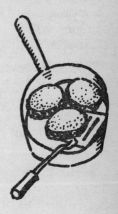

Serve them on hot buttered toast. Or buy 2 large round soft rolls; cut these into 2 halves, toast them and fill with the cooked hamburgers.

Stuffed jacket potatoes

Potatoes are more interesting and become a more complete meal if you stuff them.

You will need:

old potato	1 large
bacon	1 rasher
tomato	1
salt	pinch
pepper	shake

These ingredients will make 1 serving.

You will use:
scrubbing brush, knife, cloth, fork, chopping board, baking tray, kitchen scissors, frying-pan or saucepan, teaspoon, basin, serving plate.

1 To cook the potato allow approximately 2 hours in a very moderate oven (325°F, 160°C, or gas mark 3) *or* 1¼–1½ hours in a moderately hot oven (400°F, 200°C, gas mark 6).

2 Scrub potato well, cut out any eyes and dry with a cloth. Prick the potato with a fork to prevent the skin from bursting as the potato cooks.

3 Put on to the oven shelf, or on a baking tray. This makes it easier to take out of the oven. Cook the potato until it feels soft.

4 Remove the rind from the bacon and cut the bacon into tiny pieces; fry for a few minutes, add the tomato, also chopped. Fry for a minute more.

5 Take the cooked potato out of the oven, holding it in a tea towel so you do not burn your fingers. Cut a slice off the top, scoop out the pulp with a teaspoon, put it into a basin and mash with a fork.

6 Mix with the bacon, the tomato, a pinch of salt and a shake of pepper.

7 Pile the mixture back into the potato case, and heat for 10 minutes in the oven.

Another way to make jacket potatoes interesting

Use 25–50 grammes (1–2 oz) grated Cheddar cheese at stage 6 instead of bacon and tomato, and mix this with the mashed potato, salt and pepper. Then continue as stage 7.

Bird in a nest

In this recipe an uncooked egg is put
into the centre of the mashed potato.
It is a good idea to leave the potato
to cool a little longer than usual so
you can handle the hot vegetable, for
you need to scoop out nearly all the
centre pulp from the jacket potato.

You will need:

old potato	1 large
salt	pinch
pepper	shake
butter or margarine	25 grammes (1 oz)
milk	1 tablespoon
egg	1

These ingredients will make 1 serving.

You will use:
scrubbing brush, knife, cloth, fork,
chopping board, baking tray,
teaspoon, basin, tablespoon, cup.

1 Prepare and cook the potato as
stages 1–5 on pages 64 and 65. Mix
the hot potato pulp with the salt,
pepper, half the butter or margarine
and the milk.

2 Spoon the mashed potato pulp
back into the potato case to give a
flan shape, as shown in the picture;
do make quite certain you have a
space sufficiently large to take an
egg.

3 Put the filled potato back on to the
baking tray. Test carefully to see it is
standing upright.

4 Break an egg into a cup, then pour
this into the potato case.

5 Carefully place the remaining butter or margarine over the egg; this makes sure the yolk does not become too hard on the top before it is properly set.

6 Put the potato back into a moderately hot oven (400°F, 200°C, or gas mark 6). The baking tray should be placed just above the centre of the oven. Although a choice of temperature is given for cooking the potato in stage 1, page 64, it is better to use this setting for cooking the egg. Allow approximately 10 minutes for a lightly set egg.

Toppings for jacket potatoes

The recipes on pages 64, 65 and 66 give ideas for serving a jacket potato.

You can turn the potato into a delicious dish if you serve it topped with soured cream or cottage cheese or coleslaw or baked beans or canned flaked tuna fish or sardines.

Cauliflower cheese

This makes a cauliflower into a complete meal.

You will need:

small cauliflower	1
salt	pinch
water	about ¹/₂ litre (1 pint)

for the sauce:

cheese	50–100 grammes (2–4 oz)
flour	25 grammes (1 oz)
salt	pinch
pepper	shake
milk	¹/₄ litre/250 ml (¹/₂ pint)
butter or margarine	15–25 grammes (¹/₂–1 oz)

for the topping:

grated cheese	1 tablespoon
breadcrumbs (see page xii)	1 tablespoon

to garnish:

chopped parsley	1 teaspoon

These ingredients will make 3–4 servings

You will use:
vegetable knife, flameproof serving dish, measuring jug, saucepan, grater, plate, basin, wooden spoon, milk saucepan, colander, tablespoon, teaspoon.

1 Light the gas burner or switch on the hotplate.

2 Prepare the cauliflower by removing outside green leaves, and washing cauliflower thoroughly (leave whole). Choose an ovenproof serving dish that just fits the cauliflower and allows it to stand upright when cooked. It must also be large enough to take the sauce without overflowing.

3 Cook cauliflower in boiling salted water until tender.

4 While it is cooking, prepare the cheese sauce and topping; warm the serving dish.

5 To make the sauce, grate the cheese on to a plate.

6 Mix the flour with salt and pepper in a basin.

7 Gradually add a quarter of the milk, stirring with a wooden spoon until you have a smooth paste.

8 Put the rest of the milk into a saucepan and bring to boiling point. Take care it does not boil over.

9 Pour the boiling milk over the flour mixture, stirring all the time to prevent lumps forming.

10 Tip the sauce back into the pan and put over a low heat. Stir until the mixture boils. Then continue boiling for 3 minutes, stirring all the time. Add the butter.

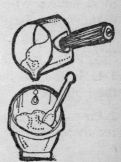

11 When stirring a sauce, make sure that the wooden spoon scrapes across the bottom and into the corners of the pan. If the sauce becomes a little lumpy, remove pan from the heat, beat the sauce with the wooden

spoon, or better still with a hand
whisk, until it becomes smooth.

12 Add the cheese – do not cook the
sauce again.

13 Strain the cauliflower.

14 Put the cauliflower into the
serving dish, switch on or light the
grill. If you cook and serve this dish
quickly, you keep more of the
important Vitamin C that is in
cauliflower.

15 Pour the cheese sauce carefully
over the top of the cauliflower.

16 Sprinkle on the cheese and
crumbs; brown for about 3 minutes
under the grill.

17 Add chopped parsley and serve at
once.

Other ways to use a cheese sauce

A cheese sauce, made as stages 5 to
12, can be poured over other cooked
vegetables; it is especially good over
cooked carrots.

You can also make a cheese sauce
and serve it with cooked fish fingers.

On pages 72–3 is a recipe for
macaroni cheese, which makes a very
good dish for dinner or supper.

Using cooked vegetables

If you have cooked vegetables left over in the refrigerator, you can turn them into an interesting main dish with the help of a cheese sauce.

1 Make the sauce as stages 5–12 in the recipe on pages 69 and 70.

2 Add the vegetables to the sauce and heat for a few minutes.

3 Spoon into a heated serving dish and garnish with a sliced tomato or parsley.

Macaroni cheese

This is a very filling dish for supper or dinner, and makes a complete meal if you cook a vegetable to have with it or make a salad.

You will need:

water	¾ litre/750 ml (1½ pints)
macaroni	75 grammes (3 oz)
salt	½ level teaspoon

for the cheese sauce, see pages 69–70.

for the topping:

grated cheese	2 tablespoons
soft breadcrumbs (see page xii)	2 tablespoons

to garnish:

parsley	few small pieces

These ingredients make 3–4 servings.

You will use:
measuring jug, 2 large saucepans, fork, grater, basin, wooden spoon, sieve, mixing bowl, pie dish.

1 Light the gas burner or switch on the hotplate.

2 Bring the water to the boil. Add the salt and put in the macaroni. You may need to break this into convenient-sized pieces. When the water returns to the boil, lower the heat and cook until the macaroni is tender but *not* too soft. Thin macaroni takes approximately 7 minutes, thick macaroni 20 minutes. To test if cooked, press one piece of macaroni against the side of the saucepan with a fork; it will break if cooked. —

3 While the macaroni is cooking, make the cheese sauce as pages 69–70, stages 5 to 12.

4 Stand a sieve in a mixing bowl and strain the macaroni.

5 Tip the macaroni into the sauce, mix well, then put into the pie dish.

6 Sprinkle grated cheese and breadcrumbs over the top.

7 Either put under the grill for 3–5 minutes to brown or towards the top of a moderately hot oven (400°F, 200°C, or gas mark 6) for 15 minutes.

8 Garnish with small pieces of parsley.

Toad-in-the-hole

This is a very good way to turn
sausages into a family supper dish.

You will need:
sausages (large are
best) 4–8
dripping or fat 15 grammes (¹/₂ oz)

for the batter:
flour (preferably 100 grammes
plain) (4 oz)
salt pinch
egg 1
milk ¹/₄ litre/250 ml
(¹/₂ pint)

These ingredients will make 4 servings.

You will use:
sieve, large basin, cup or small basin,
wooden spoon, Yorkshire pudding
tin, knife, fish slice, serving dish.

1 Sieve the flour and salt into a large
basin.

2 Break the egg into a cup or small
basin and pour into the flour.

3 Add about ¹/₄ of the milk and stir
carefully with a wooden spoon until
the flour is blended with the egg and
milk.

4 Beat really hard until you have a
thick smooth mixture. It is now called
a thick batter.

5 Some people like to let the thick
batter stand before adding the rest of
the liquid; others add the liquid
straight away. Whichever method
you use, pour the rest of the liquid
into the thick batter very slowly,

74

beating all the time. When the liquid has nearly all been put in, you may like to change the wooden spoon for a flat whisk. The important thing is to beat well so that the batter does not become lumpy.

6 When all the liquid has been added, let the batter stand in a cool place until you are ready to use it.

7 Set your oven to 425°F, 220°C or gas mark 7.

8 Grease the bottom of your Yorkshire pudding tin; the picture shows an ideal tin to use for this.

9 Put in the sausages and bake for 10 minutes towards the top of a hot oven.

10 Give the batter a final beat if it has been standing; pour it over the sausages.

11 Put back into the hot oven, but this time in the centre of the oven, to make sure the toad-in-the-hole cooks evenly at the top and bottom Cook for a further 25–30 minutes, turning the heat down to moderate after 15 minutes to prevent burning.

12 Lift out of the tin and serve as quickly as possible after cooking. The batter can take the place of potatoes, but for a complete dinner serve with a vegetable such as carrots. For supper, toad-in-the-hole could be served with tomatoes or salad

Golden rules for making a good batter

1 Allow plenty of time for the oven to heat. With an electric oven the light goes out when the right temperature has been reached; in a gas oven allow 15–20 minutes pre-heating (this is the term used for heating the oven before you cook).

2 Weigh and measure the ingredients carefully so you have the right consistency for the batter ('consistency' is the word to describe the thickness of the mixture).

3 Whisk the batter well before cooking; see stage 10 on page 75.

4 Check the cooking progress as stage 11 on page 75.

5 Making salads

A good salad depends on the ingredients being fresh. Arrange the ingredients in a bowl or on a flat dish or plate, either in a definite pattern or so that many varied colours are seen. As well as the ingredients below you can use fruit and nuts in salads.

To prepare the usual ingredients for salads:

Lettuce. Wash carefully, pulling the leaves apart. Either dry by shaking in a salad shaker or strain away surplus moisture and put on to a folded tea towel and press gently.

Watercress. Should be washed very carefully in a basin of cold water. Tear off any yellow bits.

Mustard and cress. Use a small amount at a time. Cut away from roots with scissors, hold between finger and thumb and wash. Discard seeds.

Tomatoes. If firm they need not be skinned; just wash and wipe dry. To remove the skins: put the tomatoes into a basin of boiling water for $\frac{1}{2}$ a minute. Lift out and put into cold water. Take out of the water and pull away the skin. Slice or halve, or cut into wedges.

Cucumber. Leave the skin on if you wish, or peel thinly with a knife or a potato peeler. Cut into wafer-thin slices, put on to a plate or shallow dish, and add a little salt, pepper and vinegar.

Radishes. Remove stalk and root from base, wash and dry well; slice, if you wish.

Spring onions. Remove outer skin and roots, cut away surplus green tops, wash and dry well.

Raw carrots. These should be scraped if they are young, or peeled if old. Rub against a coarse grater. Cut cooked carrots or other vegetables into neat pieces, and add to salads.

What are les crudités?

This is the name given by the French to a dish of raw vegetables. Les crudités are often served as the first course of a meal in France.

In addition to the salad ingredients mentioned on pages 77 and 78 you could be given florets (small sprigs) of raw cauliflower and red and green pepper.

When you have a pepper you cut and eat the outer flesh but you do not eat the core and seeds in the middle; these are thrown away.

The raw vegetables are generally served on a large dish with a bowl of dressing. This could be bottled mayonnaise or salad dressing but the nicest dressings are made by blending a good salad oil with lemon juice or vinegar.

This is called *French dressing*.

1 Put ¹/₂–1 teaspoon French mustard with a pinch of salt and a shake of pepper into a basin, gradually blend in 4 tablespoons olive oil or corn oil or any good salad oil.

2 Whisk or stir in 2 tablespoons of lemon juice or vinegar. The nicest vinegar to use is a white or red wine vinegar. The dressing is then ready, although many people like to add ¹/₂– 1 teaspoon castor sugar, so taste and decide if you would like a sweeter flavour. Serve in a bowl or sauce boat.

Hard-boiled egg salad

You will need:

eggs	2
lettuce leaves	4–6
tomatoes	2

These ingredients will make 2 servings.

You will use:
saucepan, tablespoon, basin, salad shaker or tea towel, serving plate or dish, chopping board, sharp knife, spoon.

1 Hard-boil the eggs and cool them (see pages 9–10).

2 While the eggs are cooking, prepare the lettuce leaves (see page 77). Arrange on a plate or dish.

3 Cut the tomatoes into slices or quarters, arrange on the lettuce.

4 Cut the shelled eggs into halves or quarters and put on top. Add mayonnaise, if wished.

Cheese salad

You will need:

lettuce leaves	4–6
tomatoes	2
cheese	50–100 grammes (2–4 oz)

These ingredients will make 2 servings.

You will use:
salad shaker or tea towel, serving plate or dish, chopping board, sharp knife, grater, large plate.

1 Make the salad base in just the same way as for an egg salad, see page 80.

2 You can put the piece of cheese on the salad, but it looks nicer if you grate it. Stand the grater on a fairly large plate.

3 Pile the grated cheese neatly in the centre of the salad, see picture.

4 If you wish, you can use a hard-boiled egg as well as the cheese, and add mayonnaise.

More cheese salads

Cheese blends very well with fruit, so serve slices of apple, orange or rings of canned pineapple in the salad. Apple goes a bad colour quickly, so spread a little mayonnaise or salad dressing over each slice.

All kinds of cooked vegetables may be added to a cheese salad; carrots. potatoes and peas are very good.

Dates, or other dried fruit, and nuts can be added to cheese in a salad; try them with cream cheese or cottage cheese for a change.

Making tomato roses

Only do this if you are used to sharp knives. Choose a firm tomato and a small pointed knife.

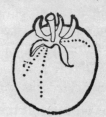

Make a cut downwards in the centre

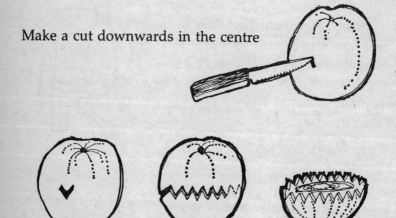

Now make a second cut upwards

Continue like this

Pull the halves apart

Mixed salad

This is the kind of salad you can serve with cold meat or cold fish or cheese.

You will need:

lettuce leaves	4–6
tomato	1
cucumber	small piece
hard-boiled egg	1
radishes, etc.	a few

to serve:
salad dressing or mayonnaise

These ingredients will make 2 servings.

You will use:
salad shaker or tea towel, chopping board, sharp knife, plate or salad bowl.

1 Prepare the salad ingredients as on pages 77–8.

2 Arrange on a flat plate, in a dish or a salad bowl.

3 Serve with either a salad dressing or mayonnaise.

Coleslaw

A coleslaw is the name given to a salad made with the heart of cabbage. The ideal type of cabbage for this is known as white or Dutch cabbage, but the heart of any crisp young cabbage could be used.

1 Wash the cabbage in cold water and dry as page 77 under lettuce.

2 Shred the cabbage very finely. There are various ways of doing this:
a You could use a sharp knife and cut the cabbage on a chopping board.
b If more convenient, rub the cabbage against the shredding side of the grater.
c Many mixers and food processors have an attachment to shred cabbage, but a grown-up should show you how to fix and use this.

3 Put the cabbage into a basin, add a little mayonnaise, then any other ingredients, such as:
a Peeled and grated raw carrot.
b Diced unpeeled eating apple (mix this with a little lemon juice to prevent the apple turning brown in colour).
c Finely chopped celery.
d Sultanas or seedless raisins and/or chopped nuts.

You can of course use all the ingredients **a** to **d** with the cabbage.

Interesting salad mixtures

A salad can be varied in very many
different ways. Pages 77 to 84 give
the way to prepare and serve the
more usual salad ingredients. Do not
imagine these are the only salads you
can make; fruits of all kinds blend
well with the other ingredients. Try
making coleslaw with red cabbage for
a change. Use other green vegetables,
such as Brussels sprouts, cauliflower
and young spinach leaves in salads.

Bacon and spinach salad

Wash, dry and shred young spinach
leaves; put into a salad bowl. Fry or
grill several rashers of bacon until
they are crisp, cut into pieces with
kitchen scissors then sprinkle over
the spinach. The bacon is nicer if it is
slightly warm. This salad looks very
pretty if you hard-boil 1 or 2 eggs,
shell and chop them and sprinkle the
yellow and white egg over the salad.

Bean salad

Mix together cooked green beans
(French or sliced runner); canned
baked beans and well-drained canned
red beans. Serve on crisp lettuce.

Orange and cottage cheese salad

Peel 1 orange for each person, or ask
an adult to cut away the peel, so
cutting the white pith off at the same
time. Cut the whole orange into rings
and put on to lettuce. Top with
cottage cheese.

6 Making puddings

Good puddings and desserts make such a lot of difference to a meal, and you will be very popular if you can make them well.

In many sweets the main ingredient is fruit. This should not be overcooked. Test with the tip of a knife.

To stew fruit

This is cooking fruit gently in a syrup of sugar and water:

1 Use the same amount of fruit, sugar and water as for fruit purée.

2 Put the sugar and water into the saucepan and bring gently to the boil. This dissolves the sugar. Remove from heat.

3 Prepare the fruit, and put it into the sugar and water 'syrup'.

4 Cook gently until tender but still whole. Hard fruit like apple slices take about 12–15 minutes, soft fruit like blackberries about 6–8 minutes.

5 The fruit can be served hot or cold with custard or fresh cream.

Fruit purée

By this method the fruit becomes quite smooth and you can use it with ice-cream or to make fruit snow (see page 89).

You will need:

*prepared fruit**	225 grammes (8 oz)
water: with soft juicy ripe fruit	4 tablespoons
with hard firm fruit	8 tablespoons
sugar	25–40 grammes (1–1½ oz)

These ingredients will make 2 servings.

You will use:
tablespoon, saucepan, wooden spoon, sieve, basin.

1 Put the ingredients into a saucepan over a very low heat.

2 Cook, stirring often, until you have a smooth thick mixture.

3 Put a sieve over the basin and rub the fruit through with the wooden spoon if you wish to remove skins or pips.

*This means peeled and sliced apples or halved and stoned plums, or use raspberries, blackberries, gooseberries or other soft fruit.

Fruit snow

This is a very delicious cold dessert made from fruit purée

You will need:

fruit purée (see previous page)	⅛ litre/125 ml (¼ pint)
egg white	1

to decorate:

glacé cherries or *angelica*	2 piece

These ingredients will make 2 servings.

You will use:
2 basins, whisk, tablespoon, glasses or serving dish, knife.

1 Make the fruit purée (see page 88) and let it become quite cold.

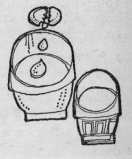

2 Separate the egg white from the yolk. You do this by cracking the egg and allowing the white to drop into one basin and the yolk into another. Another way is to break the egg carefully on a plate. Then put an eggcup over the yolk and pour the white into a basin.

3 Stand the basin on a folded tea towel to keep it steady and use an egg whisk to whip the egg white until it is very stiff and stands in peaks when you take the whisk out. The egg yolk is not used in this recipe but could be added to scrambled eggs (see pages 50–51).

4 Add the white to the fruit purée and fold together. Turn the metal spoon *gently* and *slowly* to mix the egg white and fruit. If you are too rough you lose the light texture.

5 Put into glasses or a serving dish.

6 Decorate with small pieces of glacé cherry or angelica.

Whisking egg whites

In order to whisk the white of an egg it must be separated carefully, so that there is no yolk (see stage 2, page 88), and the basin and whisk must be dry and free from any grease.

There are various kinds of egg whisks that can be used.
a A flat whisk.
b A balloon
    whisk.
c An electric
    whisk.

Whisk the white until it stands in peaks; if you continue whisking the white becomes dry and crumbly.

Fruit salad

There are many ways of making a
fruit salad. The easiest is to use
canned and fresh fruit together.

You will need:

apricots, pineapple or peaches	1 small can
grapes	a few
orange	1
banana	1
eating apple	1
ripe pear	1

*These ingredients will make 3 servings
or 4–5 with ice-cream as well.*

You will use:
can opener, basin, plate, knife,
serving dish.

1 Open the can of fruit, pour the
syrup into a basin. Put the fruit on a
plate, cut into neat pieces; add to
syrup.

2 Halve the grapes, remove the pips.
Peel the orange, take out segments of
fruit and remove the skin and pips.*

3 Peel banana, apple and pear and
cut into neat pieces. Do this just
before serving so that they keep a
good colour.

4 Mix the fresh fruit with the canned
fruit and syrup; put into serving
dish.

*This is quite difficult to do. If you
find you are breaking the orange
segments then just take out the pips

91

and leave the skin, or ask a grown-up to help you.

In summertime you can add other fruit such as cherries, raspberries, etc., to the fruit salad.

To serve with fruit salad

You can serve cold custard sauce, made according to the instructions on the custard powder tin. When you have made the custard pour it into a serving bowl or jug. Cut a circle of greaseproof paper to fit the top of the jug or bowl, make it quite damp and put it over the top of the custard. As the custard cools the damp paper prevents a skin forming. Or you can serve ice-cream with the fruit salad, or fresh cream in a jug.

Fruit salad tarts

Make the pastry as pages 117 and 118; roll out and cut into rounds as given under jam tarts, page 119. Bake the pastry as for jam tarts but without a filling. When the tarts are cold fill with fresh fruit salad.

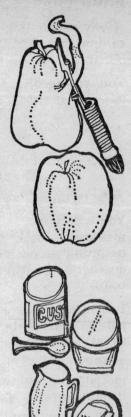

Fruit jelly

A jelly makes a light pudding. You can put the jelly into 4 dishes at stage 3 if you prefer.

You will need:

water	approx. ¹/₂ litre/500 ml (approx. 1 pint – see jelly packet)
fruit jelly	¹/₂ litre/500 ml (1 pint) packet

These ingredients will make 4 servings.

You will use:
measuring jug, kettle or saucepan, basin to dissolve jelly, tablespoon, another basin or mould, serving plate or dish.

1 Heat the water and dissolve the jelly as instructed on the packet; cool slightly.

2 Rinse out a ¹/₂ litre (1 pint) basin or mould with cold water. This helps in turning out the jelly.

3 Pour the jelly into dishes or mould and leave in a cool place to set. If putting into the refrigerator, make sure the liquid is no longer steaming.

4 To turn out:
a Put a serving plate or dish in clean cold water and shake it nearly dry. This will enable you to move the jelly into the right position on the dish without breaking it.
b Dip the mould into warm water for 5 seconds to loosen jelly.
c Put the plate over the top of the mould. Hold firmly and turn over so

that the plate is now under the
mould. Shake gently and lift away
the mould.

To make jelly more interesting

a Add 2 sliced bananas to the cooled
jelly at stage 1.
b Open a small can of mandarin
oranges or other fruit, strain off the
juice from the can and add enough
water to make up to the ½ litre (1
pint) or as given on the packet. Heat
and use this at stage 1, then add the
fruit to the cooled jelly.

Harlequin jellies – for a party

Make 2 or 3 different flavoured
jellies, allow to set in separate basins.
When firm cut into neat squares and
put into individual glasses.

Milk jelly

This makes an interesting change from an ordinary fruit jelly and is more nourishing.

You will need:

fruit jelly	½ litre/500 ml (1 pint) packet
hot water	⅛ litre/125 ml (¼ pint)
milk	approx. ⅜ litre/375 ml (approx. ¾ pint)

These ingredients will make 4 servings.

You will use:
kettle or saucepan for small quantity of water, measuring jug, basin, tablespoon, mould, serving dish.

1 Dissolve the jelly as instructed on the packet, but use only ⅛ litre/125 ml (¼ pint) of water.

2 *Allow to cool* but not to set, then stir in the cold milk to give ½ litre/500 ml (1 pint) of jelly liquid.

3 Pour the milk jelly into a mould. Leave to set and turn out.

Ice-cream and hot chocolate sauce

An easy way to make a special sweet with ice-cream.

You will need:

ice-cream	2 portions
bar plain chocolate	50 grammes (2 oz)
water	1 tablespoon

These ingredients are for 2 servings.

You will use:
basin, saucepan, tablespoon, 2 serving dishes or sundae glasses.

1 Light the gas burner or switch on the electric hotplate.

2 Half fill the saucepan with cold water and stand the basin over this.

3 Break the chocolate into small pieces and put into the basin with the water.

4 Put on to the heat and leave until the chocolate has melted.

5 Arrange the ice-cream in glasses.

6 Spoon the chocolate sauce over the ice-cream.

This recipe can very easily be turned into the following party dessert:

Chocolate walnut sundae

You will need:
ice-cream, chocolate sauce, a few walnuts.

You will use (for this and the sundae below):

2 or 3 large spoons, sundae glasses, a chopping board and knife, basins and forks.

1 Put vanilla, coffee or chocolate ice-cream into sundae glasses or any pretty bowls you may have and top with chocolate sauce made as page 96.

2 Sprinkle over a few chopped nuts or leave the nuts whole.

Fudge walnut sundae

Buy 50 grammes (2 oz) vanilla or other flavoured fudge, put this into a basin.

Either stand the basin over a saucepan of hot water (make sure the basin balances safely) and leave until the fudge has melted, or ask a grown-up to show you how to melt the sauce in a microwave cooker. Use the melted fudge instead of chocolate sauce.

Another chocolate sauce

If you have no chocolate you can make a good sauce with cocoa and other ingredients.

You will need:

margarine	15 grammes ($^1/_2$ oz)
cocoa	2 level tablespoons
golden syrup	2 level tablespoons
water	2 tablespoons

These ingredients will make 2 servings.

You will use:
saucepan, tablespoon, wooden spoon.

1 Put all the ingredients for the sauce into a small pan and heat until the margarine and cocoa have quite dissolved.

2 *Stir well* all the time. Use as the chocolate sauce on page 96.

There is a variation on the sauce above. This produces a sauce with a more delicate flavour.

Use 25 grammes (1 oz) butter or margarine, 1 level tablespoon cocoa, 1 level tablespoon chocolate powder, 2 tablespoons sugar, 2 tablespoons water. Heat the ingredients as in the recipe above.

Fruit sundae

You will need:
fresh fruit such as strawberries, raspberries or sliced bananas (kept white by sprinkling with lemon juice) *or canned fruit, ice-cream, ready set jelly* (see page 93), *double cream.*

You will use:
utensils as page 97.

1 Put a layer of the fresh or well-drained canned fruit into a sundae glass, top with some ice-cream.

2 Whisk the jelly in a basin with a fork, put into glass, then add the rest of the ice-cream.

3 Whip the cream in another basin and spoon on to the top of the sundae, then decorate with a piece of fruit.

To whip cream

Choose double cream. Pour it into a basin, then whisk hard with a fork or a hand or rotary whisk until it stands up in peaks.

Baked apple

When you bake an apple in the oven you keep all the flavour of the fruit. Follow the directions in stages 2 and 3 carefully.

You will need:
cooking apples   2 medium or large

This will make 2 servings.

You will use:
apple corer or potato peeler, ovenproof baking dish, sharp knife.

1 The apples can be cooked in a very moderate oven (325°F, 160°C or gas mark 3). Allow 50 minutes–1 hour for small to medium apples, 1–1¼ hours for large apples; or cook for approximately 35–40 minutes for small to medium, 40–50 minutes for medium to large apples in a moderately hot oven (375°–400°F, 190°–200°C, or gas mark 5–6).

2 Wash and dry the apples and remove the centre core with an apple corer or potato peeler. Stand in ovenproof baking dish.

3 Slit the skin round centre with the tip of a sharp knife to prevent it bursting in cooking.

Stuffed baked apples

A stuffing makes the apples more interesting. The apples can be filled before baking with any of the following. The amounts are enough for 2 large apples.

a 4 teaspoons dried fruit and 4 teaspoons sugar.
b 4 teaspoons brown sugar topped with 25 grammes (1 oz) butter.
c 2 tablespoons bramble jelly.
d 2 tablespoons golden syrup.

To stuff the apples:

Core as stage 2 on page 100, put the apples into the baking dish, spoon the filling into the centre holes and cook as stage 1 on page 100.

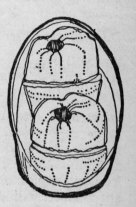

Baked apples served cold

Although most people may prefer eating baked apples hot, they are extremely good served cold. The skin wrinkles and looks slightly unappetizing, so remove this from the warm apple and brush the fruit with a little melted apricot jam.

Fruit crumble

A nice pudding to eat hot. We have used apples here but you could use plums or other fruit.

You will need:

fruit	225 grammes (8 oz)
water	1–2 tablespoons
sugar	25 grammes (1 oz)

for the crumble:

flour (plain or self-raising)	50 grammes (2 oz)
margarine	25 grammes (1 oz)
sugar	25 grammes (1 oz)

These ingredients will make 2 servings.

You will use:
sharp knife, basin, strainer, small pie dish, plates for sugar, flour and margarine, sieve, mixing bowl, tablespoon.

1 Set your oven to 375°F, 190°C or gas mark 5.

2 Prepare the fruit; peel apples and cut into thin slices, keep in a basin of cold water until ready to use, to keep as white as possible, then strain away the water.

3 Put the prepared fruit into a small pie dish – about ¼ litre/250 ml (½ pint) size.

4 Sieve flour into a mixing bowl; some people like to add a pinch of salt.

5 Add the margarine and rub in as described on page xii; add the sugar.

102

6 Sprinkle the crumble mixture over the fruit and press down with the tips of your fingers; make sure no crumbs of flour, etc., are on the rim of the dish (see picture).

7 Bake in the centre of a moderate oven for 25 minutes. While this pudding is cooking make custard sauce (see page 92) to serve with it, or have cream.

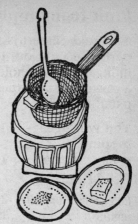

Other flavours for a crumble

Coconut crumble. Add 25 grammes (1 oz) desiccated coconut to the flour mixture at stage 5, after adding the sugar.

Rolled oat crumble. Use only 25 grammes (1 oz) of flour and 25 grammes (1 oz) rolled oats – the kind used to make porridge. Increase the sugar slightly; use 40 grammes (1½ oz). Add the rolled oats to the flour mixture at stage 5, after adding the sugar.

Pink foam apples

This cold dessert is very good for a party. To pour out the evaporated milk, make two holes in the can with a can opener or open the can in the usual way.

You will need:
topic:

evaporated milk	1 small can
rose hip syrup	2 tablespoons
large sweet apples	2
lemon juice	1 tablespoon
seedless raisins	2 tablespoons
rose hip syrup	2 tablespoons

These ingredients will make 4 servings.

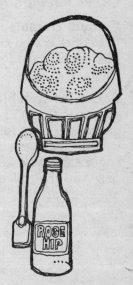

You will use:
can opener, large basin, whisk, tablespoon, small sharp knife, large plate, lemon squeezer, 4 dishes.

1 Make the topping: pour the evaporated milk into a basin and whisk until it is like thick cream. You will find this quite hard work, so stop during whisking for a few minutes if your arm aches.

2 Stir in the first 2 tablespoons of rose hip syrup.

3 Peel, quarter and core the apples and slice them very thinly on to the plate.

4 Pour over the lemon juice, then turn apple slices over.

5 Arrange the apple slices in the four dishes, top with raisins.

6 Spoon over the rest of the rose hip syrup, allow to stand for a few minutes.

7 Spoon over the topping.

Another cold dessert made like this

You can use fresh pears instead of apples and you could use fresh double cream instead of evaporated milk.

More flavours for the sauce

Cassis is the name given in France to a blackcurrant flavouring. You can buy a cassis (blackcurrant) syrup. Use this instead of rose hip syrup in the recipe on page 104. Raspberry and strawberry syrup are sold to flavour milk shakes, and these can also be used instead of rose hip syrup.

No-bake blackberry betty

This makes a very good autumn pudding.

You will need:

cooking apples	225 grammes (8 oz)
blackberries	225 grammes (8 oz)
sugar	50 grammes (2 oz)
water	1 tablespoon

crumb mixture:
butter	50 grammes (2 oz)
fresh white breadcrumbs (see page xii)	150 grammes (6 oz)
soft brown or Demerara sugar	50 grammes (2 oz)

to decorate:
uncooked ripe blackberries	a few

These ingredients will make 6 servings.

You will use:
sharp knife, 2 saucepans, wooden spoon, tablespoon, glasses or glass dish.

1 Light the gas burner or switch on the hotplate.

2 Peel and slice the apples.

3 Gently stew the apples, blackberries and sugar together with 1 tablespoon water until the fruit is tender; stir once or twice.

4 Melt the butter in another saucepan. Remove from the heat and mix in the crumbs and sugar with the spoon.

5 Fill glasses or a glass dish with alternate layers of fruit and crumb mixture, finishing with a layer of crumb mixture.

6 Leave to stand for a few hours, preferably overnight.

7 Decorate with raw blackberries, and serve by itself or with cream, ice-cream or custard.

Fruit is tender when it feels soft if tested with the tip of a knife.

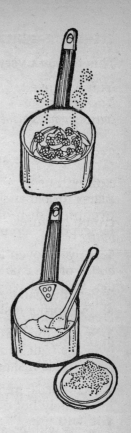

Other fruits to use

Rhubarb. Use 450 grammes (1 lb) rhubarb. Cut this into neat pieces of about 3.5–5 cm (1½–2 inches) in length. Cook as stage 3 on this·page.

Raspberries. Use 450 grammes (1 lb) raspberries. Do not cook but mash with 50 grammes (1 oz) sugar, then proceed as stage 4 to 7 above.

Baked bananas

A new way of serving bananas.

You will need:

bananas	2 large or 4 small
butter or margarine	25 grammes (1 oz)
brown sugar	2 tablespoons

These ingredients are for 2 servings.

You will use:
plates for bananas, sugar and butter,
ovenproof dish, flat knife,
tablespoon, serving dishes.

1 Set your oven to 375°–400°F, 190°–200°C or gas mark 5–6.

2 Peel the bananas and put them into an ovenproof dish.

3 Spread the butter or margarine over the fruit and sprinkle with the sugar. This makes a sauce.

4 Bake for 20 minutes in a moderately hot oven.

5 Serve with cream, ice-cream or custard.

Orange baked bananas

You may now make a more interesting pudding by adding orange juice.

You will need:
Ingredients as baked bananas plus 1 large orange.

1 Squeeze the juice from the orange.

2 Prepare the oven and bananas as stages 1 and 2 on page 108.

3 Spread the butter over the fruit and sprinkle with the sugar, then add orange juice.

4 Cook and serve as stages 4 and 5 on page 108.

Coconut bananas

Prepare the bananas as the recipe above, but add a sprinkling of desiccated coconut over the fruit at stage 3 after adding the orange juice to the dish. Cook as stage 4 on page 108.

7 Tea time

It is very pleasant and not too difficult to prepare the food for tea. Here are some of the things that go to make up a really good tea.

Sandwiches. Recipes are given on pages 34–40; cut these smaller for tea than for a picnic or supper snack.

Scones. Either buy these or make them. Serve with butter and jam. You will find the recipe for scones on pages 113–16. Or cut slices of bread and butter and serve with jam.

Cakes. There are many recipes on pages 124–8.

Tea. Serve with milk and sugar; younger children may like milk or lemonade.

If you are planning a 'high tea', you can include a more substantial dish, either some kind of salad, see pages 77 to 86, or savoury, see pages 41 to 76.

Laying the table for tea

1 Put a cloth on the table, lay a small plate and knife for each person, with a napkin.

2 Add cups and saucers, teaspoons, a jug of cold milk, the sugar basin and a mat or stand for the teapot.

3 Arrange the sandwiches on a plate; make these look pretty with parsley or washed lettuce leaves.

4 Either cut the scones across the middle and spread with butter and jam, or serve them whole on a plate with butter in a dish (you will need a butter knife) and jam in a dish with a spoon.

5 If you are serving bread and butter cut it *carefully*. Cut the loaf downwards on the bread board with the bread knife, so you cannot cut yourself. Spread the bread with butter. You need a rounded knife, not a sharp knife, for this.

6 Arrange the slices or halved slices neatly on a plate.

7 Put the cakes on a plate; some people like to use a doily.

8 If you are having a 'high tea', you will need large knives and forks, and heat-resistant mats under the plates if the food is hot.

9 Make the tea and carry it in carefully. You can also have a spare jug of boiling water to fill up the teapot. Stand this on a mat.

Tea on a tray

Many people do not like a 'sit-down' tea.

Arrange the cups and saucers on a tray with the teaspoons, jug of milk and sugar basin. You can cover the tray with a traycloth if you wish.

Carry in the small plates, knives (if needed) and napkins, also the plates of food.

Do *not* attempt to put the teapot on the tray; carry in the tray, *then* the teapot, *then* the hot water.

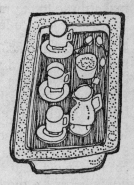

Always put teapots and jugs of very hot water in a safe place away from small children.

Little children like small pieces of food, so cut bread and butter into small squares; make very small scones, cakes and biscuits.

Plain scones

You will need:

self-raising flour (*or plain flour and 1* *level teaspoon baking* *powder*)	100 grammes (4 oz)
salt	pinch
margarine or butter	15–25 grammes (½–1 oz)
milk	approx. 4 tablespoons

These ingredients will make 4 scones.

You will use:
mixing bowl, sieve, wooden spoon,
tablespoon, palette knife, flour sifter,
pastry board, rolling pin, baking tray,
wire cooling tray, serving plate.

1 Set your oven to 425°F, 220°C or
gas mark 7.

2 Place the bowl on the table, put the
sieve over this, then push either the
self-raising flour and salt, *or* the plain
flour, salt and baking powder
through the sieve into the bowl; use
the wooden spoon.

3 Rub the fat into the flour with the
tips of your fingers (see page xii).

4 Add 2 tablespoons of milk; mix
with the flour and fat, using a palette
knife. Add another tablespoon of
milk and mix again. You will find
that the dough is beginning to come
together. For this quantity of flour
you will need approximately 4
tablespoons of milk, but add the
fourth tablespoon very slowly so that
you do not put in too much.

113

5 The dough is ready when it will form a ball and leave your mixing bowl clean.

6 Put down the palette knife and use the tips of your fingers to gather the dough together.

7 Shake a little flour from the flour sifter or flour dredger on to your pastry board and shake a small amount of flour over the rolling pin.

8 Roll out the scone dough gently and firmly into a thick round, as shown in the picture. If the edges of the round get untidy, just neaten them with your hands.

9 When you have a neat round, mark this into 4 sections.

10 This is ready to go on to the baking sheet or baking tray. A plain scone like this could be baked on an ungreased baking tray, but some people prefer greasing the tray. Put the scone on the tray – it is then ready to be baked.

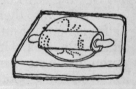

11 A whole scone round, as this is called, should be baked just above the middle of the oven.

12 Bake the scone round for approximately 20 minutes.

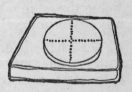

13 If you separate the 4 sections into triangles (see picture); you could bake them towards the top of the oven, as they cook more quickly.

14 Lift from the baking sheet or tray on to a wire cooling tray.

15 Serve scones hot or cold, with butter and jam.

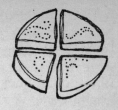

Note! You can also cut the scones into small rounds with a pastry cutter, after you have rolled out the dough at stage 7. These round scones should be baked on a tray near the *top* of the oven for 10–12 minutes.

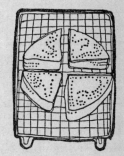

Successful scones

a Make sure the oven is really hot before the scones are put in to cook – see stage 1, page 113.
b Try to make the scones as quickly as possible; avoid handling the mixture more than necessary.

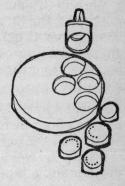

Other kinds of scones

A sweet scone. Add 1 tablespoon of sugar to the flour and fat mixture at stage 3, or instead of sugar use 1 tablespoon honey, golden syrup or black treacle; you will then need less milk, and will have to grease the baking tray (see page x).

Fruit scones. Add 1 tablespoon of sugar and 1 tablespoon or 25 grammes (1 oz) dried fruit – currants, sultanas, or mixed fruit – to the rubbed-in mixture at stage 3.

Cheese scones. Sieve $\frac{1}{4}$ level teaspoon salt, a shake of pepper and a pinch of dry mustard with the flour at stage 2. Rub in the margarine, add 25 grammes (1 oz) finely grated cheese, then mix with the milk. You will need to grease the baking tray (see page x).

Oatmeal scones. Use half rolled oats and half flour instead of all flour. Use 50 grammes (2 oz) plain flour, sieve this with $\frac{3}{4}$ level teaspoon baking powder and a pinch of salt. Rub in 15–25 grammes ($\frac{1}{2}$–1 oz) of margarine or butter, then add 50 grammes (2 oz) of rolled oats. Proceed as the recipe on pages 113 to 115 or flavour the scones as suggested above.

Note! Wheatmeal or granary flour can be used instead of ordinary plain flour in scones.

Making shortcrust pastry

Pastry is not easy to make, so it is better to leave this until you have practised rubbing in on easier things like scones.

You will need:

plain flour	100 grammes (4 oz)
salt	pinch
margarine	50 grammes (2 oz)
cold water	approximately 1¼ tablespoons

You will use:
mixing bowl, sieve, wooden spoon, plate, knife, tablespoon, palette knife, flour sifter, pastry board, rolling pin.

1 Place the bowl on the table, put the sieve over it, then push the flour and salt through the sieve into the bowl; use the wooden spoon for this.

2 Put the margarine on a plate and cut it into small pieces.

3 Add the margarine to the flour and rub this in with the tips of your fingers (see page xii).

4 Add *nearly* all the water, mix the ingredients together with the palette knife, then put this down and use your fingertips to gather the dough together. You may well find you need to use a little more of the water to make the dough roll into a ball and leave the mixing bowl clean.

5 Shake a little extra flour from the flour sifter on to the pastry board and rolling pin, then roll out the dough to the required shape and thickness; see below.

Note! Instead of 50 grammes (2 oz) of margarine, you may use 25 grammes (1 oz) margarine and 25 grammes (1 oz) of lard or cooking fat.

To roll out shortcrust pastry

Rolling is a very important part of pastry making.

1 Gently pat the pastry dough to make it into a good shape.

2 Press the floured rolling pin down on to the dough and roll away from you, making the pastry a thinner and longer shape. *Do not* roll backwards and forwards or turn the rolling pin in all directions.

3 If the pastry is becoming too long a shape, lift it carefully, turn it at right angles and roll. Continue like this until you have the right shape and thickness of pastry.

Jam tarts

1 Make and roll out the shortcrust pastry as pages 117 and 118. It should be a good 0.5 cm (1/4 inch) in thickness.

2 Take a tray of patty tins (sometimes called bun tins) and find a pastry cutter that is just a little bigger than the diameter (measurement across) of the small patty tin; you need to allow extra pastry because of the depth of each patty tin. If you do not have a pastry cutter then use the top of a cup or glass, but handle this carefully, for it could break.

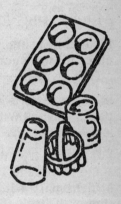

3 Cut out 6–9 small rounds to fit into the patty tins. The number made will depend upon the size of the patty tins you use.

4 You may not be able to cut out all the rounds from the first pastry shape, so carefully fold over the pieces left after cutting out the rounds, then re-roll this and cut out more rounds.

5 Fit the pastry rounds into the patty tins; press down gently but firmly with your fingers.

6 Put a teaspoon of jam into each pastry case. Do not use too much jam, for it would bubble out during cooking and burn.

7 Place the tray of patty tins just above the centre of a moderately hot to hot oven (400–425°F, 200–220°C or gas mark 6–7) for 10–12 minutes or

until the pastry is golden in colour.

8 Allow the small tarts to cool for 2–3 minutes in the tins, then lift out and place on a wire cooling tray if you want them to be served cold. If serving hot, put on to a serving plate.

Note! If you think there is too little jam for a good filling add a small extra amount to each tart while they are warm.

More fillings for tarts

Instead of using jam you can use other fillings such as lemon curd or golden syrup.

In some cases it is better to make the pastry shapes without a filling. This is called 'baking blind'.

Put the pastry into the patty tins as stage 5 on page 119; prick the bottom of the pastry with a fork then bake as stage 7. Check after 8–9 minutes to make sure the pastry is not becoming too brown.

When the pastry is cooked you could fill it with fruit, as suggested on page 92, or with cream or cottage cheese and chopped nuts.

Rock buns

Simple-to-make buns for tea. They are crisp and sweet and extra nice if you eat them when fresh.

You will need:

self-raising flour	100 grammes (4 oz)
margarine	50 grammes (2 oz)
caster sugar	50 grammes (2 oz)
dried fruit	50 grammes (2 oz)
egg – very small	1

to give a shiny top:

sugar	1–2 teaspoons

These ingredients will make about 5–6 buns; if using the metric measurements you have a smaller quantity.

You will use:
baking tray, pastry brush, sieve, mixing bowl, basin, fork, palette knife, 2 teaspoons, saucers or plates for sugar and dried fruit, wire cooling tray, serving plate.

1 Set your oven to 400°–425°F, 200°–220°C, gas mark 6–7.

2 Grease a baking tray; page x tells you how to do this.

3 Sieve the flour into a mixing bowl, so there are no lumps. If you find only plain flour in the cupboard, then sieve 1 *level* teaspoon baking powder with the flour so your cakes rise well.

4 Rub in the margarine with the tips of your fingers; the sketch shows how this is done.

5 Add the sugar and dried fruit.

121

6 Break the egg into the basin and beat the egg with a fork. Add to the rest of the ingredients in the mixing bowl; if it was a large egg, then do not use it all. Add it slowly.

7 Mix with the knife until the cake dough stands up in points; see the picture.

8 If you have any egg left, put it into a small cup and cover with 1 tablespoon cold water; later you can add it to scrambled eggs.

9 Put 5–6 equal-sized 'heaps' on to the baking tray, allowing space for them to spread. Use 2 teaspoons for this.

10 Sprinkle lightly with a little sugar.

11 Bake towards the top of a moderately hot to hot oven for 10–15 minutes.

12 The cakes are cooked when they are light golden brown in colour and when they feel quite firm as you touch the sides.

13 Lift very carefully with the palette knife on to the wire cooling tray. If you cannot find a tray like this, then use the grid from the grill pan of your cooker.

Now you have made rock buns successfully you can make some more cakes like them, as I suggest in the following three recipes.

Lemon buns

1 Grate the yellow part of the rind from the lemon on to a plate. The picture shows you how this is done.

2 Add this to the flour in the recipe for rock buns; as you see, a clean brush is the best thing to take the rind from the grater.

3 Make the buns just like rock buns.

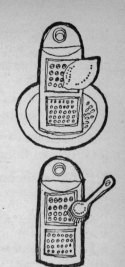

Coconut rock buns

Use the same ingredients as rock buns, plus 2 level tablespoons desiccated coconut, which you add at stage 5.

Jam buns

1 You use the same mixture as for rock buns but you do not use dried fruit.

2 Instead you use 1 tablespoon jam.

3 As well you need an extra teaspoon of flour.

4 Put a teaspoon of flour on a plate.

5 Make the cake mixture as for rock buns (see pages 121–3), but do not use quite as much egg, so you can take small pieces of the dough and roll it into balls with your fingers, as in the picture.

6 Put on the greased baking tray, just as rock buns.

7 Dip your finger in the flour, then press into the centre of each bun to make a hollow.

8 Put a little jam into this, using two teaspoons, then pull the edges of the cake mixture over the jam.

9 Sprinkle with sugar if desired, and bake as before.

Funny face cakes

Special cakes for a party. Choose luxury margarine that creams quickly.

You will need:

self-raising flour	100 grammes (4 oz)
caster sugar	100 grammes (4 oz)
easy creaming margarine	100 grammes (4 oz)
eggs	2

for soft glacé icing:

sieved icing sugar	300 grammes (10 oz)
lemon juice	about 3 tablespoons

to decorate:
'Smarties' or 'polka dots', angelica, currants, chocolate vermicelli

These ingredients will make about 24 cakes; if using the metric measurements you have a smaller quantity.

You will use:
mixing bowl, sieve, wooden spoon, teaspoon, paper cake cases, patty tins, wire cooling tray, basin, tablespoon, serving plate.

1 Set your oven to 400°F, 200°C or gas mark 6.

2 Sieve dry ingredients into a bowl. Add the other ingredients and beat together for 2 minutes until well mixed.

125

3 Spoon this mixture into about 24 cake cases, arranged in patty tins to keep their shape.

4 Bake above the centre of a moderately hot oven for about 15 minutes. Allow to cool.

5 Sieve the icing sugar and add the lemon juice by degrees, stirring well, until you have a thick icing. Spoon over the cakes.

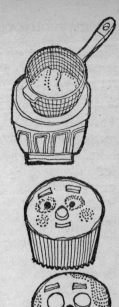

6 Decorate the cakes with the 'polka dots', currants, etc., to make faces, as shown in the picture.

Cup cakes

There is no need to ice the cakes to look like 'faces'. You can simply make the icing as stage 5 on this page and spoon over the cakes. The icing can be mixed with water instead of lemon juice.

Note! Soft wheat sponge flour can be used in place of self-raising flour.

Easy creaming ('soft' or 'luxury') margarine, should be kept in the refrigerator until ready to use.

Chinese chews

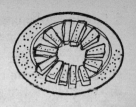

These fruit cakes are excellent for a special picnic or party. Chop the dates and nuts carefully or ask a grown-up to do this.

You will need:

margarine or butter	25 grammes (1 oz)
caster sugar	75 grammes (3 oz)
egg	1
vanilla essence	½ teaspoon
self-raising flour	50 grammes (2 oz)
dates	75 grammes (3 oz)
walnuts	25–50 grammes (1–2 oz)

to decorate:

icing sugar	25 grammes (1 oz)

These ingredients will make 12 small fingers.

You will use:
sandwich tin, mixing bowl, wooden spoon, small basin, fork, teaspoon, 3 plates for flour, dates and walnuts, tablespoon, sieve, chopping board, sharp knife, palette knife, small sieve or strainer for icing sugar, serving plate.

1 Set your oven to 375°F, 190°C, or gas mark 5. Grease a 20 cm (8 inch) sandwich tin as page xiii and sprinkle with a little flour.

2 Cream the margarine and sugar as page xii.

3 Break the egg into a basin.

4 Measure the vanilla essence carefully, add to the egg, beat with a fork.

5 Gradually beat into the margarine and sugar.

6 Spoon the flour into a sieve and shake into the margarine mixture.

7 Chop the dates and nuts and add to the flour, etc.

8 Spread into the tin and bake for approximately 15 minutes above the centre of a moderate oven.

9 Cool in the tin, then cut into small fingers, coat in icing sugar, and lift out.

10 The easiest way to coat the fingers is to rub the icing sugar through a small strainer or sieve.

Peach and lemon squares

These can be served for tea or as a new kind of pudding.

You will need:
for the crumb crust:

butter	75 grammes (3 oz)
digestive biscuits	150 grammes (6 oz)
caster sugar	50 grammes (2 oz)
ground cinnamon	good pinch

for the filling:

peach slices	1 large can
lemon	1

to decorate:

sliced fresh lemon	1
or *crystallized lemon slices*	12

These ingredients will make 12 squares.

You will use:
basin, wooden spoon, rolling pin, 2 sheets greaseproof paper, baking tin (see stage 4), can opener, strainer, basin, 1 tablespoon, 3 plates, sharp knife, fork, grater, 1 teaspoon, serving dish.

1 Set your oven to 350°F, 180°C or gas mark 4.

2 Cream the butter with the wooden spoon until it is soft.

3 Crush biscuits to fine crumbs between two sheets of greaseproof paper.

4 Stir into the butter with the sugar and cinnamon and press just over half into a 30 cm × 20 cm (12 inch × 8 inch) tin, greased as page x.

5 Drain the juice from the canned peaches into a basin and lift out the peach slices.

6 Reserve 12 slices for decoration and chop the remainder with a knife and fork.

7 Finely grate the lemon rind.

8 Halve the lemon, take out the lemon pulp with a spoon and chop this with the knife and fork.

9 Mix the chopped lemon and grated rind into the chopped peaches on the plate.

10 Spread this mixture over the crumb crust base.

11 Sprinkle with the remaining crumb crust mixture.

12 Press down lightly with the tips of your fingers.

13 Bake for 35–40 minutes in the centre of a very moderate oven, then chill in the tin.

14 Cut into 12 squares, decorate each square with a peach slice and half a lemon slice or a crystallized lemon slice.

15 Serve cold with ice-cream and the juice from the peaches.

Variations

Use apricots instead of peaches

Use cooked, well-drained, apple slices.

Biscuit crust flan

The ingredients used to make the base of the peach and lemon squares on page 129 can be used to make an uncooked flan case. Omit the pinch of ground cinnamon.

Follow stages 2 and 3 on page 129, then add the biscuit crumbs to the creamed butter and sugar.

Mix with your hands then press the mixture into a 15–18 cm (6–7 inch) flan dish.

Chill for several hours in the refrigerator; do not bake

Fill with ice-cream and fresh fruit just before serving.

Vanilla biscuits

You will need:

self-raising flour	100 grammes (4 oz)
margarine or butter	50 grammes (2 oz)
sugar	50 grammes (2 oz)
vanilla essence	few drops
milk	1–2 teaspoons

to sprinkle over biscuits:
sugar   1 teaspoon

These ingredients will make 10–12 biscuits; if using the metric measurements you have a smaller quantity.

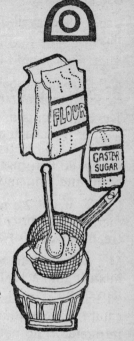

You will use:
plates or saucers for the flour, margarine and sugar, sieve, mixing bowl, palette knife, skewer, cup, teaspoon, pastry board, rolling pin, sharp knife, 2 baking trays, fork, wire cooling tray, serving plate.

1 Set your oven to 350°–375°F, 180°–190°C or gas mark 4–5.

2 Sieve the flour into a mixing bowl.

3 Rub in the margarine with your fingertips or with the forefinger and thumb of each hand until it is like crumbs. Add the sugar.

4 To take a few drops of essence, dip the skewer into the bottle, take it out, let the drops fall into a cup and add 1 teaspoon milk.

5 Pour the milk and vanilla into the biscuit mixture.

6 Knead the mixture very hard with your fingers; page xii tells you about kneading.

7 The mixture should form a ball. If too dry, add another teaspoon of milk. This should be enough.

8 Put on to the pastry board and divide into about 10–12 equal-sized pieces.

9 Roll pieces into neat balls.

10 Place on 2 ungreased baking trays with plenty of room for them to spread out.

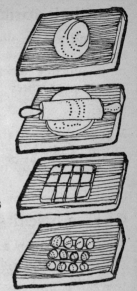

11 Flatten slightly with the back of the fork or with your hand.

12 Sprinkle the sugar over the biscuits.

13 Bake in a moderate oven, near the centre, for about 15 minutes until golden.

14 Lift out of the oven, cool for 5 minutes on the trays so that the biscuits do not break, then lift with a palette knife and place on a wire cooling tray.

15 When quite cold, store in an airtight tin away from bread, pastry or cakes.

Chocolate biscuits

1 Weigh out the flour as for vanilla biscuits, take away 1 level tablespoon flour, put this back in the bag.

2 Add 1 level tablespoon cocoa to the flour.

3 Sieve the flour and cocoa as stage 2 in the vanilla biscuits; continue as for the vanilla biscuit recipe.

Cheese biscuits

1 Omit the sugar and vanilla essence in the recipe for vanilla biscuits on page 132.

2 Grate 50 grammes (2 oz) Cheddar, or other good cooking cheese.

3 Sieve the flour with a pinch of salt, a pinch of dry mustard powder and a shake of pepper.

4 Rub in the margarine as stage 3 on page 132, then add the grated cheese together with milk to bind as stages 4 and 7 on page 133.

5 Continue as stages 8–15 on page 133. It is advisable, though, to grease the baking trays only very lightly when using cheese in a recipe.

8 Parties and picnics

There are plenty of recipes in this book which you can use when you give a party. Try to plan dishes that can be made well in advance. Each recipe in this book tells you how many people it serves so you will know just how much food to prepare. Allow about 3–4 sandwiches for each person.

Menu 1

Here is a menu that is ideal for a buffet-type meal where everyone helps themselves, and is suitable for tea or evening time.

Mixed and open sandwiches (pages 34–40).
Peach and lemon squares (pages 129–31).
Fruit salad (pages 91–2), with ice-cream.
Fruit cup (pages 32–3).

Preparations:
1 Make the peach and lemon squares earlier in the day or the day before the party; keep in a cool place.

2 Make the fruit salad. Keep the dish covered.

3 Make the fruit cup.

4 Prepare the sandwiches, arrange on plates and cover them with foil or clingfilm, or a barely damp, clean tea towel, so that they do not dry. The refrigerator is an ideal storage place.

5 Arrange the food and drink on the table with plates, glasses and napkins. You will need spoons for the fruit salad.

Menu 2

Here is another good buffet menu, best for small numbers because you must toast the sandwiches just before you eat them, and this would be rather hectic for a lot of servings.

Hot toasted cheese club sandwiches (pages 39–40).
Ice-cream.
Coffee (pages 22–3).

Preparations:
1 Arrange the table, make the coffee, put out plates and spoons for the ice-cream.

2 Have the bread and filling ready so that all you have to do at the last minute is the toasting.

Menu 3 – for a winter party

It is fun to have some really hot food for a party in wintertime. You could choose a menu similar to menu 1, and open tins of soup to heat and serve hot. If you prefer to make some hot dishes, here are two very easy menus.

Stuffed jacket potatoes (pages 64–5).
Hot sausages, grilled or fried (page 61)

136

Fruit jellies (pages 93–4) with cream.
Rolls, butter, and cheese.
Coffee and fruit drinks.

Preparations:
1 Make the jellies in the morning or
the day before so they set.

2 Prepare the jacket potatoes and
cook them completely if you wish so
they are just ready to heat, or get
everything prepared, i.e., bacon, etc.,
cooked so the last-minute
preparations are soon made.

3 Cook the sausages by grilling or
frying. You can also cook them in a
greased tin in the oven, when they
take about 30–35 minutes.

4 Arrange the table, make the coffee
and fruit drinks.

Here are two recipes for summer
parties and picnics, when most of us
enjoy cool refreshing food.

Menu 4 – for a summer party

Cheese salad and egg salad (pages
81–2 and 80).
Rolls and butter.
Pink foam apples (pages 104–5) and
vanilla biscuits (pages 132–3).
Cold milk, fruit drink.

Preparations:
1 Make the vanilla biscuits several
days before the party if wished and
keep in an airtight tin.

2 Make the pink foam apples; allow
plenty of time for this as it is quite a
slow recipe.

3 Prepare the salads on plates or

dishes and cover with foil or clingfilm so they do not dry.

4 Put out the cold drinks, etc., and lay the table.

Menu 5 – for a summer party

Cold sausages with hard-boiled eggs (pages 10 and 61), tomatoes, lettuce.
Cheese scones (page 116) and butter.
Chinese chews (pages 127–8) and fresh fruit.
Lemonade (pages 30–31).

Preparations:

1 Make the Chinese chews earlier in the day or even the day before; keep in an airtight tin.

2 Make the cheese scones the day of the party so they are fresh.

3 Make the lemonade.

4 Cook the sausages and eggs and shell the eggs; prepare the lettuce.

5 Arrange the food on plates and trays and take into the garden.

If you wish to use this menu for a picnic then:

1 Carry the Chinese chews in a tin so they do not break.

2 Split the scones, spread with butter and then wrap them or put in a tin.

3 Pour the cold lemonade into a vacuum flask.

4 Cook the sausages and eggs, shell the eggs, wrap in foil or clingfilm or put into plastic picnic boxes.

Special treats

A party gives an opportunity to make special treats. In addition to the suggestions on pages 135 to 138 there are a number of ideas in this book you can use for a special treat.

On the next page is a recipe for iced lollies. Home-made lollies are delicious and, if you use fresh fruit juice or purée, they are good for you too.

Points to remember

If sieving fruit for an iced lolly or for the fruit purée on page 88, it is advisable to use a nylon or hair sieve. Metal sieves discolour fruit.

If you have a waste disposal unit be very careful when preparing food for cooking that you do not allow any utensils to go down the unit, and never touch it with your fingers.

Iced lollies

In order to make iced lollies you need to buy special moulds. While these vary slightly – some are made in metal, others in plastic – every type of iced lolly has a stick with which to hold the iced dessert. If made of plastic, wash after use; wooden ones have to be replaced.

Iced lollies with fruit juice

Use fresh, canned or bottled orange juice, or canned or bottled grapefruit, apple or pineapple juice. Add a little sugar if you must, but remember that too much sugar is not good for you.

1 Put the lolly mould into the tray, put the sticks in position; then carefully fill the moulds with the juice.

2 Place in the freezer or freezing compartment of the refrigerator and leave for about 1¹/₂–2 hours.

3 Remove the lollies from their moulds.

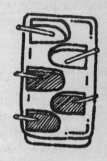

Iced lollies with fruit purée

Make a purée of uncooked ripe raspberries, strawberries or blackberries by rubbing the fruit through a sieve or putting it into a liquidizer or food processor. Add a little sugar to taste. Continue as stages 1 to 3 above.

Index

apple, baked 100;
  stuffed 101
apple fruit cup 33
apples, pink foam 103–4

bacon and apple rings 15
bacon and egg, fried 11–12
Bacon and fried bread 16
bacon and sausages:
  fried 59; grilled 58
bacon and spinach
  salad 85
bacon and tomato 14–15
baked bean sandwiches 48
baked beans, sweet and
  sour 48
baking xii
bananas: baked 108;
  orange baked 109;
  coconut bananas 109
bean chowder 48
bean salad 85
beans on toast 47
beating xii
bird in a nest 66–7
biscuit crust flan 131
biscuits 132–4
blackberry betty 105–6
blending xii
boiled egg 9–10
boiling xiii

Boston baked beans 49
breadcrumbs, making x
breakfast 1–18; in bed 17–
  18
buns 121–4

cakes 124–8
cauliflower cheese 68–70
cheese biscuits 134
cheese club sandwich,
  toasted 39
cheese dreams 54–5
cheese on toast 43
cheese salad 81–2
cheese sauce 68–70
cheese scones 116
Chinese chews 127–8
chocolate biscuits 134
chocolate drinks 25–7
chocolate milk shake 27
chocolate sauce 96–8
chocolate walnut
  sundae 97
cocoa 26
coconut crumble 103
coconut rock buns 123
coffee, making 22–3;
  iced 24
coleslaw 84
cooking, methods of xii–
  xiii

141

omelette 52–3
open sandwiches 38
orangeade 30
orange and cottage cheese
 salad 86
orange baked bananas 109

party, having a 135–40
pastry, shortcrust 117–18
peach and lemon squares
 129–31
picnics 137–40
pink foam apples 104–5
porridge 6
potatoes, stuffed
 jacket 64–5
puddings 87–109
purée, fruit 88

rock buns 121–4
rolled oat crumble 103
rose hip milk shake 28
rubbing in xii

salads 77–86
sandwiches 34–40
sandwich fillings 35
sardine rarebit 46
sardines on toast 56
sauces: cheese 68–70;
 chocolate 96, 98;

fruit 104–5
sausages 60; for a party 61
scones 113–16
simmering xiii, 19
spaghetti with cheese 42
stewed fruit 87
sundaes 97–9
symbols xiv

tea time 110–34
tea (beverage),
 making 20–1
toad-in-the-hole 74–6
toasted sandwiches 39–40
tomato roses 82
tomato Welsh rarebit 45
tomatoes on toast 42
tools for cooking ix–xi

vanilla biscuits 132–3
vegetables in cheese
 sauce 71

warming xiii
Welsh rarebit, 44–6
whipped cream 99
whisked xii, 90

yogurt drinks 28
Yorkshire rarebit 46

Edited by Biddy Baxter
The Blue Peter Book of Gorgeous Grub 95p

When the *Blue Peter* BBC television programme launched its Gorgeous Grub
competition, children sent in 33,250 of their own favourite recipes. Here
are the forty prizewinners, a collection of mouth-watering gorgeous grub! A
part of the publisher's profits from the sale of this book were donated to the
International Year of the Child.

Margaret Powell
Sweetmaking for Children £1.25

Toffee, fudge, marzipan – nothing tastes as good as real home-made sweets!
Join in the fun as Margaret Powell explains in this amusing and practical
guide how everything is done, from choosing the utensils to decorating the
finished goodies – not forgetting of course her five golden rules for safety
in the kitchen.

Katie Stewart
A Young Cook's Calendar 75p

Month-by-month recipes and cooking ideas compiled especially for children.

Anni Axworthy
Crazy Cook £1.25

Invisible ink picture puzzle book

A whole feast of picture puzzles for you to solve. The answers are invisible
but your magic pen will make them appear. Help Crazy Cook with a
Muddled Milkshake, a Bread Baffler, a Tart Tease and a Pizza Puzzle. Open
the book and see what's on the menu – and don't forget to come to Crazy
Cook's party! Fun for everyone from four up.

Piccolo non-fiction you will enjoy

○	**Sweetmaking for Children**	Margaret Powell	£1.25p
○	**The Body Book**	Claire Rayner and	
		Dr Hugh Jolly	£1.95p
○	**Bananas Don't Grow on Trees**	Joseph Rosenbloom	90p
○	**Top to Toe: Good Grooming for Girls**	Rubie Saunders	80p
○	**Skulls**	Richard Steel	£1.00p
○	**A Child's Bible: New Testament**	Shirley Steen	£2.95p
○	**A Young Cook's Calendar**	Katie Stewart	75p
○	**Have You Started Yet?**	Ruth Thompson	£1.00p
○	**The Big Book of Facts**		£2.95p
○	**Junior Jet Club Captain's Log**		£1.50p
○	**Secrets of the Human Body**		£1.50p

All these books are available at your local bookshop or newsagent,
or can be ordered direct from the publisher. Indicate the number of
copies required and fill in the form below   11

....

Name_____
(Block letters please)

Address_____

_____

Send to CS Department, Pan Books Ltd,
PO Box 40, Basingstoke, Hants
Please enclose remittance to the value of the cover price plus:
35p for the first book plus 15p per copy for each additional book
ordered to a maximum charge of £1.25 to cover postage and
packing
Applicable only in the UK

While every effort is made to keep prices low, it is sometimes
necessary to increase prices at short notice. Pan Books reserve the
right to show on covers and charge new retail prices which may
differ from those advertised in the text or elsewhere